MOLIERE TODAY – 2

CONTEMPORARY THEATRE REVIEW
AN INTERNATIONAL JOURNAL

Editor in Chief
Franc Chamberlain, Nene College, Northampton, UK

Editorial Board
Leon Gitelman (Russia)
Malcolm Knight (UK)
Jacques Lecoq (France)
Judith Malina (USA)
Neville Shulman (UK)
Anatoly M. Smeliansky (Russia)
Maria Delgado (UK)

Aims and Scope
Contemporary Theatre Review is an international journal concerned with all aspects of theatre – from text-based drama and current developments worldwide, to work of an interdisciplinary or cross-cultural nature. The journal includes primary material, production notes, documents and interviews as well as research. **Contemporary Theatre Review** complements the companion **Contemporary Theatre Studies** book series.

Notes for contributors can be found at the back of the journal.

© 1997 OPA (Overseas Publishers Association) Amsterdam B.V. Published in The Netherlands by Harwood Academic Publishers, a member of The Gordon and Breach Publishing Group. All rights reserved.
Reprinted by Routledge,
2 Park Square, Milton Park, Abingdon, Oxon, OX14 4RN

Transferred to Digital Printing 2004

Except as permitted under national laws or under the photocopy license described below, no part of this publication may be reproduced or transmitted in any form or by any means, electronic, mechanical, photocopying or otherwise, or stored in a retrieval system of any nature, without the advance written permission of the Publisher.

World Wide Web Addresses
Additional information is also available through the Publisher's web home page site at http://www.gbhap.com. Full text on-line access and electronic author submissions may also be available.

Editorial enquiries by e-mail: <editlink@gbhap.com>.

Ordering Information
Four issues per volume. Subscription are renewed on an annual basis. 1997 Volume(s): 6–8

Orders may be placed with your usual supplier or at one of the addresses shown below. Journal subscriptions are sold on a per volume basis only. Claims for nonreceipt of issues will be honored if made within three months of publication of the issue. See Publication Schedule Information. Subscriptions are available for microform editions; details will be furnished upon request.

All issues are dispatched by airmail throughout the world.

Subscription Rates Base list subscription price per volume: ECU 67.00*. This price is available only to individuals whose library subscribes to the journal OR who warrant that the journal is for their own use and provide a home address for mailing. Orders must be sent directly to the Publisher and payment must be made by personal check or credit card.

Continued

Continued

Separate rates apply to academic and corporate/government institutions. Postage and handling charges are extra.

*ECU (European Currency Unit) is the worldwide base list currency rate; payment can be made by draft drawn on ECU currency in the amount shown or in subscriber's local currency at the current conversion rate set by Publisher. Subscriber's should contact their agents or the Publisher. All prices are subject to change without notice.

Publication Schedule Information: To ensure your collection is up-to-date, please call the following numbers for information about the latest issue published: +44 (0) 118-956-0080 ext. 391; +1 973 643-7500 ext. 290; or web site: http://www.gbhap.com/reader.htm.
Note: If you have a rotary phone, please call our *Customer Service* at the numbers listed below.

Orders should be placed through one of the addresses below:

IPD Marketing Services,
PO Box 310
Queen's House, Don Road
St. Helier, Jersey
Channel Islands JE4 0TH
Telephone: +44 (0) 118-956-0080
Fax: +44 (0) 118-956-8211

PO Box 32160
Newark, NJ 07102, USA
Telephone: +1 800 545-8398
Fax: +1 973 643-7676

Kent Ridge, PO Box 1180
Singapore 911106
Republic of Singapore
Telephone: +65 741-6933
Fax: +65 741-6922

Yohan Western Publications Distribution Agency
3-14-9, Okubo, Shinjuku-ku
Tokyo 169, Japan
Telephone: +81 3 3208-0186
Fax: +81 3 3208-5308

Enquiries can also be sent by e-mail: <info@gbhap.com> and the world wide web: http://www.gbhap.com.

Rights and Permissions/Reprints of Individual Articles
Permission to reproduce and/or translate material contained in this journal must be obtained in writing from the Publisher.

This publication and each of the articles contained herein are protected by copyright. Except as allowed under national "fair use" laws, copying is not permitted by any means of for any purpose, such as for distribution to any third party (whether by sale, loan, gift, or otherwise); as agent (express or implied) of any third party; for purposes of advertising or promotion; or to create collective or derivative works. A photocopy license is available from the Publisher for institutional subscribers that need to make multiple copies of single articles for internal study or research purposes. Any unauthorized reproduction, transmission or storage may result in civil or criminal liability.

Copies of articles may be ordered through SCAN, the Publisher's own document delivery service. SCAN provides customers with the current contents and abstracts to all Gordon and Breach and Harwood Academic journals. Please contact one of the addresses listed above to receive SCAN, or view current contents and abstracts directly on the Web at http://www.gbhap.com, and for ordering.

The Publisher is also a member of Copyright Clearance Center.

This journal is sold CIF with title passing to the purchaser at the point of shipment in accordance with the laws of The Netherlands. All claims should be made to your agent or the Publisher.

Published in The Netherlands

Contents

The Other Voice and the Script: Re-Viewing Classical French Theatre   1
Laurence Romero

Molière's Dom Juan Adapted for Brecht's Berliner Ensemble   13
Peter W. Ferran

Changing the Limits: Molière, Planchon, and *L'Avare*   41
Helen L. Harrison

Getting Down to Business in Molière's *Le Bourgeois Gentilhomme*   57
Philip R. Berk

Notes on Contributors   77

Index   79

    83

The Other Voice and the Script: Re-Viewing Classical French Theatre

Laurence Romero

One of the major challenges in teaching classical seventeenth-century French theatre today is to discover contemporary resonances in these texts while respecting their own time and place. Since the ultimate destination of all drama/script is theatre and since recent innovative French theatre directors have written extensively on their works, their stage writing and mises en scene are excellent sources for renewing the classics today. This essay argues for the value of such production materials for any contemporary understanding of the classics and offers examples from stagings of Molière's *Tartuffe* and *Dom Juan*, and of Racine's *Bérénice*.

KEY WORDS: Molière, Racine, Roger Planchon, Contemporary stagings of the classics, Post-war French stage directors, Teaching classical French theatre today.

For teaching Molière and classical French theatre today, a broad spectrum of methods and materials is available from the critical literature, pedagogical investigations, and theatre praxis. The real task in renewing teaching techniques, in re-teaching the classics from the seventeenth-century, is to develop strategies that connect with innovative directions in academic research and especially in theatre production, like Patrice Chéreau's radical recasting of Molière's *Dom Juan* as a critique of the ancien régime in its confrontation with libertinism. As we teachers and critics begin to inform our critical discourse with innovative ideas and perspectives from stage practice, the argument becomes more compelling that theatre texts can no longer be dealt with adequately through conventional literary exegesis unconnected to stage production. Indeed, a full appreciation of drama as theatre necessitates integrating some aspect of mise-en-scène, be it staging tradition or the provocative implications of contemporary stage writing (*écriture scénique*), the conceptual framework of mise-en-scène. Along with academic criticism, connecting theatre praxis to the dramatic literature program provides a source for new pedagogical strategies through the incorporation of uncommon materials like reviews and analyses of innovative stagings, and the notes and commentaries of stage directors themselves.

The best and most imaginative of these theatre artists have been in the forefront not only of staging new authors but in the indispensable continuous renewal of the classics. It is they, the stage directors, who provide the "other voice", adding perceptions beyond the text/script that link it to the total visual, material, and verbal experience which is theatre. As examples will illustrate later, there is a significant gap between understanding and appreciating a play in light of innovative contemporary stagings, and having merely read it and the literary criticism on it. Knowing precisely the function of the "Exempt" in the denouement of *Tartuffe*, flavoring the preening opportunistic careerism rampant at Louis XIV's court when *Bérénice* was originally written and produced, grasping the concept and role of the salon in *Le Misanthrope*, feeling the repressive ambience of the ancien régime society that surrounds the anti-hero of *Dom Juan*, these and similar insights can color greatly one's perception of these plays. While none of these points is naturally embedded in the script and immediately obvious to spectators today, they were brilliantly displayed in the mises-en-scène of Roger Planchon, Jean-Pierre Vincent, and Patrice Chéreau. No serious discourse, pedagogical or otherwise, should ignore this pivotal adjustment of focus when dealing with French classical theatre as it relates to us *hic et nunc*. Molière today outside the context of contemporary theatre practice is unthinkable: Molière 'offstage' is an oxymoron.

Any attempt to integrate staging materials into any critical discourse is nourished by the French "hommes de théâtre" themselves who traditionally have been expansive cultured practitioners, generating written commentaries, mise-en-scène descriptions, apologies and polemics. The names of some of the innovative stage directors since ca. 1950 are well known: Jean Vilar and Jean-Louis Barrault in the first generation, followed by Roger Planchon, Patrice Chéreau, Ariane Mnouchkine, Marcel Maréchal, Jean-Pierre Vincent, Bernard Sobel, Jérôme Savary, and the recently deceased Antoine Vitez. Some of the best practitioners of production criticism who routinely integrate mise-en-scène perspectives into their analyses are also well-known: Bernard Dort, Alfred Simon, Emile Copfermann, J. M. Piemme, and the late Gilles Sandier. From a semiotic perspective, Michel Corvin, Patrice Pavis, and Anne Ubersfeld are excellent theorists although some of their work is difficult to use pedagogically except when applied to specific mises-en-scène. Regardless of one's choices, the tools are available for adopting a production perspective and beginning to think theatrically – not only textually. Following is a descriptive narrative on three groups of directors and then on aspects of a few contemporary mises-en-scène to illustrate how theatre practice can and should intervene in any modern re-viewing of the French classics today. While the primary focus is on Molière stagings, one Racine production will also serve the central argument.

The efforts of innovative directors in post-war French theatre beginning with Jean Vilar and the cultural decentralization around 1950 have taken many directions over the years, of which three are of particular interest to us here. Perhaps the most creative have been the theatre collectives that have literally reinvented or recreated texts through the performances of the players themselves. The best examples have come from Ariane Mnouchkine and her collective at the Cartoucherie de Vincennes, creating/performing such works as *1789* and *1793*, *L'Age d'or*, and *Les Atrides*, along with kabuki Shakespeare and the film *Molière*. Another important innovator was Antoine Vitez, especially his experimentations with stage language and gesture in the Molière and Marivaux cycles. In his highly experimental stagings of Racine's *Andromaque* and *Phèdre*, at once cerebral and theatrical, Vitez had the players deconstruct the classical alexandrine and recompose it in a sycopated continuum of "parole et gestuelle", seeking new sense and meaning from the interplay of the gestural and the symbolic. "Les acteurs deviennent alors les servants d'un jeu et ils interviennent pour décrire ce jeu, les lieux imaginaires, et raconter le fil de l'histoire. ... Nous pensons que ce type de mise-en-scène doit permettre une compréhension plus vive du texte de Racine et susciter des idées et des images qui resteront dans la mémoire des spectateurs liées – fussent-elles contemporaines – à Racine et au vers alexandrin". ["Here the actors serve a playing process and they intervene to describe the playing field, the imaginary loci, and to recount the train of the story. We believe that this type of staging should provide a more vivid understanding of the text and elicit ideas and images of Racine and the alexandrine verse – even if contemporary – that will remain in the memory of the spectators."] (Vitez, 1991: 333–334). The project was not an attempt at problematizing the text itself but rather its referents deep in Racine's language. Unfortunately creative stagings like those of Vitez and Mnouchkine, somewhat abstract although visually arresting on stage, do not lend themselves easily to seminar discussions, unless one were to project videos of them and undertake a study of their specific theatricality.

The most serviceable production materials are from the third group of innovative directors, those who seek not to reinvent or analyse script language per se but rather its historical referents, the time, the context, and the subtexts of the script. Their stage writings remind one of aspects of New Historicism "avant la lettre", in that they are sensitive to the historicity of the text and the textuality of history as well as to the interplay of culture and history. While the works of these directors (Planchon, Chéreau, Maréchal, Savary, Sobel, Vincent, etc.) are very different, they share a common ambition: the will to re-imagine the classics in light of contemporary epistomologies and to cast their stagings within a frame of current sensibilities, our own "bienséances". Patrice Chéreau's bold staging of Molière's *Dom Juan* in 1969 broke with a long staging tradition that projected the protagonist as a profligate lover and religious hypocrite, in line with the Spanish source. Chéreau brought the play back to its authentic roots and imagined seventeenth-century French aristocratic society confronting a rebel from its own ranks. Torn by inner contradictions and not very noble, this Dom Juan is nevertheless a fanatical "libre esprit", determined to confound the norms of paternity, marriage, religion, and the civil order of his day. Here is part of Chéreau's reasoning: "Voici une époque troublée où les grands se sont beaucoup battus pour avoir le pouvoir mais l'ont perdu. L'un d'entre eux, qui s'appelle Don Juan, se fait libertin et met au pillage la société morale ... le libertinage étant de ses morales progressistes qui poussent à la révolution sans la faire. L'auteur, qui était payé par le pouvoir ... fait apparaître une machine à tuer les libertins et, pour nous distraire, il nous raconte l'événement comme un conte de fées. Mais nous ne nous y tromperons pas". ["These were troubled times when the nobles fought hard to gain power then lost it. One of them, Don Juan, becomes a libertine and castigates society's mores ... libertinism being one of those progressive ideologies that lead to revolution without actually making it. The dramatist, who was paid by the authorities ... brings forth a machine for exterminating libertines and, to distract us, he recounts the event like a fairy tale. But we will not be fooled".] (Sandier, 20). In spite of his bravado, Dom Juan doesn't stand a chance. The forces of status-quo politics and morality conspire against him and converge in the ominous "machine à tuer les libertins". Chéreau materialized that concept by exposing heavy machinery underneath the stage, almost literally on the backs of the sweltering peasants operating the contraption in that cramped airless space. The actual stage machine of ropes pulleys, cranks, cogs, etc. was designed to recall that of a seventeenth-century theatre and to create the visual equivalent of the grinding machinations of state terrorism. While Dom Juan never actually becomes entangled in the machine, its relentless, ponderous squeaking and crunching created an air of impending doom. This highly effective theatricality was not at all gratuitous: the don's dramatic rapt into hell at the end is no longer the consequence of his immorality as in conventional interpretations of the play, but of his political libertinage. The wrath of the denouement here is not of an avenging god but of a terrorist state seeking to throttle "the progressive ideology that leads to revolution".

Not only victim, Chéreau's Dom Juan is also a traitor to his aristocratic class by continuing to profit from its privileges even while unable to bend his ill-disciplined nature to the demands of the chivalric code of conduct. Although the caste tolerates and excuses him for a time, ultimately he must be crushed to preserve the silent but implacable law of conform or perish. The hero as pariah, as Dom Juan is here, is a far cry from earlier influential productions of this play, like Louis Jouvet's, where the protagonist is seen in the throes of a personal and religious crisis. Chéreau's shift in focus to a broader historical critique of a past social order invites a richer, more complex appreciation of Molière's problematic play.

Another innovative staging in this direction was Jean-Pierre Vincent's production of Molière's *Misanthrope* in 1977, an interpretation that projected a "contre-utopie", revealing a society living only by its own signs. The décor presented a vast and sumptuous living space with a partially visible stylized grand staircase, recalling La Bruyère's famous dictum that high social life at his time – and Molière's – was lived "dans une antichambre, dans des cours ou sur l'escalier". Reading systematically against the staging tradition of Alceste as the frantic protagonist constantly bellowing and bullying, Vincent projected a quiet, determined Alceste, gently but surely making his misanthropic way through a vacuous society of small-minded, factuous hypocrites. The incredible slow pace of this production brought into sharp relief all the characters, their language and comportment, and forced us to rethink the old canards that traditionally attend a production of this play. There are of course risks in this rereading: defusing Alceste's explosive, intemperate nature immediately deflates the play's dynamic hilarity. What is left is a subtle and deeply comic – but not funny – representation of a minor class mimicking the pleasures and privileges of a grander order coming to life in Versailles under the pretentious aegis of "le Roi Soleil".

Other contemporary stagings of French classics include two particularly successful ones: Roger Planchon's stagings of Racine's *Bérénice* and Molière's *Tartuffe*. Since the 1950s, Roger Planchon has been actor, director, playwright, and company director, and since 1972 co-director of France's largest and most visible national theatre, the Théâtre National Populaire (TNP). Probably more than anyone since Jean Vilar, Planchon has been a veritable "homme de théâtre total", a model in French theatre culture set by none other than Molière himself in the 1660s. In a recent assessment of his work, Bernard Dort called Planchon "... un prodigieux brasseur de textes et d'images scéniques. Il a fait de la mise en scène une mise en épreuve de notre réalité comme de notre héritage culturel. Tout le théâtre français porte sa marque". ["... a prodigious conjurer of texts and stage images. He made of mise-en-scène a testing of our reality as well as of our cultural heritage. He has left his mark on all of French theatre".] (1989: 400). In a brief departure from his Molière stagings, let us begin with Planchon's controversial staging of Racine's *Bérénice* from 1970, the tricentenary year of the play's first production.

The traditional line of interpretation of *Bérénice* – in the theatre and in virtually all criticism and school editions – had the protagonist Titus, prince and then emperor of Rome, faithfully loving Bérénice, Queen of Palestine, and planning to marry her as he has promised for the past five years. His father recently deceased, Titus is now emperor and because of the antipathy of the Roman republican senate toward foreign nobility, Titus is made to suffer his obligations of honor and duty and to send away his beloved Bérénice, "malgré lui, malgré elle". Reading not so much against Racine's text but against the accumulated critical and staging traditions of *Bérénice*, Planchon told a very different love story. Here Titus is not the sympathetic lover-emperor responding gallantly to the exigences of "honneur, mérite, et devoir", but rather a crafty, ambitious young politician quietly determined to rule Rome and the world, and prepared, especially at the beginning of his reign, to acquiesce to the demands of the senate. Consequently, Planchon's production emphasized certain verses, especially from Titus, creating a sub-text from which the young emperor's true feelings emerge: he is in fact fatigued of Bérénice and what has been their ideal relationship, and he is more than ready to sacrifice her to his devouring ambition. But Titus is immature and deeply narcissistic and he is often emotionally confused and inconsistent even within himself. It follows that he is frightened of the steadfast queen whose honesty and guilessness expose his own insecurity, hypocrisy and deceit. In this emotional maelstrom, not only is Bérénice bewildered by Titus's strange comportement, but his own confidant Paulin does not trust his master, and the intimate friend Antiochus is without a clue as to what might happen next.

Given Titus's volubility, Planchon's stage conception sharply challenged the view of *Bérénice* as a lyrical tragedy where the protagonist-duo is made to endure equally the fate of their shared "tristesse". Planchon argued that we have taken the wily and defensive Titus too much at his word and that it is high time we understand him not by what he says but by what he does; in other words, that we come to terms with Titus – as with Tartuffe – through his "faire" and not his "dire". "Il est exact que Titus parle de son amour. Ses mots sont si bien tournés, si élégants, que l'on finirait par le croire, si tous ses actes concrets ne s'opposaient pas à ses mots et même n'en étaient pas un flagrant démenti. ... Pas une second, pas un instant, Titus n'hesite à renvoyer Bérénice ... et lorsqu'on additionne le total de ses actes, on s'aperçoit que le caractère de Titus n'est pas celui d'un amoureux mais l'inverse. Titus n'aime pas Bérénice. Peut-être l'a-t-il aimée il y a cinq ans, la pièce autorise un peu à le dire, mais lorsque la pièce commence, et c'est la seule chose importante, Titus n'aime pas ou n'aime plus Bérénice". ["It is true that Titus speaks of his love. His language is so well-turned that we would believe him were it not for the fact that his concret acts are in flagrant contradiction to what he says. ... Not for a second does Titus hesitate to dismiss Bérénice ... and when we consider all of Titus' acts we notice that his disposition is not one of a lover but the opposite. Titus does not love Bérénice. Perhaps he did five years ago, the text suggests that. But when the action begins, and that is the only important thing, Titus does not or no longer loves Bérénice".] (Copfermann: 367–370).

In spite of his fickle speech which remains oblique to the end, what Titus actually does is straightforward and unambiguous: he dismisses Bérénice summarily and forever, and tactlessly gives her to their common friend Antiochus, a man even more irresolute than Titus and for whom the queen has but a badly concealed contempt. In the substantial gap between what the emperor says and what he does, Planchon invites us to scrutinize Titus's discourse and to see it for what it is: deceptive, hypocritical, self-serving, even though moments of vague sentimentality occasionally interrupt the main thrust of the emperor's designs. In the well-known three lines from his monologue in IV, 5, beginning with "Ah! lâche! fais l'amour et renonce à l'Empire", the underlying stress is on fleeing, deception, cowardice, concealment, and on ceding to others more worthy. Might this be the true Titus, one can ask. Isn't this consistent with his comportment during the entire play? Doesn't this explain in large part his unwillingness to face Bérénice? To undermine Titus's pompous and egregious presence, Planchon's production casts him in a glaring light, not to flatter, but to expose his self-indulgence and egotism. Long rows of mirrors and bright light constantly reflect and refract Titus's appearance and every gesture, a visual proliferation that accentuates his postering and preening and reveals a persistent fatuousness. This stage metaphor is especially rich in revealing not only Titus's soul, but the character of much of courtly life around the time of Louis XIII and Louis XIV, the implicit setting of Racine's play and the explicit superimposed venue of Planchon's production.

This then is Racine's Titus for our time: an ambitious, devious young man on the move, a crass egotistical careerist prepared to say and do anything to advance politically and consolidate his power. There is no lyricism in his relationship to Bérénice, only a callousness which he is quite prepared to reveal to himself in one of his interior monologues. Titus: "Car enfin au combat qui pour toi se prépare / C'est peu d'être constant, il faut être barbare. /... il ne s'agit plus de vivre, il faut régner". ["For in your forthcoming struggle / Steadfastness is too little, severity is the order / It is no longer a question of living but of ruling".] (IV, 4).

Planchon's production of *Bérénice* from 1670 bridges the gap between past significance and present meaning, moving the script from yesterday to today, from classic to modern. Controversial to be sure, the interpretation rested solidly on a minute reading of Racine's text for which Planchon had full respect. Coherent and credible, it staged the characters today, while leaving intact yesterday's script. In foregrounding the "dire/faire" dichotomy (reminiscent of Barthes), Planchon reminds us that the "dire" approach in past conventional stagings had reduced *Bérénice* to marginal status in the modern repertory. The key innovative adjustment of focus to Titus's "faire" revealed resonances in Racine's text very compatible with contemporary sensibilities and revived the play for our time. Two subsequent innovative stagings of *Bérénice* by A. Vitez and K.-M. Grüber reconfirmed the continual need to revitalize the classics.

Another celebrated Planchon production was his mise-en-scène of *Tartuffe*. The long staging tradition of this, the most popular work in the classical repertory, had projected Tartuffe as an unctuous hypocrite "d'un certain âge", confronting a stupid, credulous, and ineffectual Orgon. Not so for Planchon. Logically, given Tartuffe's considerable success in Orgon's house and before, the man cannot be as obviously repulsive as the tradition had imagined him. Instead, Planchon casts an intelligent, relatively young and vigorous Tartuffe, not unhandsome and not without a certain occasional dubious charm. Orgon is also renewed as a man who logically cannot be so inept since he has amassed a fortune, has been involved – quietly and unhappily – in politics, and managed to win for himself a beautiful and intelligent second wife, Elmire. Orgon isn't dumb, he's obssessed, as many of Molière's comic protagonists are. In traditional stagings however, his obsession is not identified; it is depicted as an ambiguous, undirected yearning, apparently for nothing more than social success and esteem. In one of the most striking departures from the long tradition of staging and criticism on *Tartuffe*, Planchon argued that Orgon's obsession is far too deep and pervasive to be mere social ambition. The obsession is there but it has a name that no one had dared pronounce. Ours is the ideal time to bring Orgon out of the closet: his obsession is clearly for Tartuffe and it is clearly homosexual in nature. Planchon's insight here is not for scandal but a logical reading of Orgon's comportment throughout the play. Here is the director's response to a letter from a Catholic spectator troubled by his interpretation: "Admettez une seconde que j'aie raison, que mon hypothèse soit fondée. En tant que catholique elle devrait vous satisfaire puisque je montre que la fausse dévotion d'Orgon, son erreur religieuse, a un fondement extérieur à Orgon: son homosexualité latente. Ce n'est plus seulement un chrétien ridicule qui est présenté, mais un homme aveuglé par sa passion". ["Admit for the moment that I'm right and that my hypothesis is well founded. It should satisfy you as a catholic since I show that Orgon's false devotion, his religious error, has its source outside of Orgon, in his latent homosexuality. What is presented is no longer a ridiculous christian but a man blinded by passion".] (Planchon, 1975: 31). While it is a latent condition which is never on vulgar display, Orgon's homosexual urge is compelling and it influences all of his attitudes and actions. This erotic tension provides Planchon's production with an energizing metaphor around which much of the action occurs: the dramatic binary possession/dispossession. While Tartuffe lusts to possess physically and materially, and Orgon in his obsession is prepared to dispossess – and does – his entire family, other personnages also move between these two poles. For example, members of Orgon's family change clothes often to emphasize the small rituals of a rich and privileged bourgeois family, a transfer of clothing that also implies a momentary material dispossession/possession. The latter gesture opens the essentially private cycle of erotic exchange to a larger, more public sphere. And in fact Planchon's mise-en-scène makes much of Orgon's rich bourgeois existence and evokes, beyond the family anecdote, the rise of a wealthy new bourgeois class attached to and committed to the rise of an ambitious young king. Literary history recalls that Louis XIV reached his kingly majority in 1661, that Molière's three versions of *Tartuffe* evolved between 1661–1669, and that the ban on the play was lifted by written license from the king himself in early 1669, upon petition from the playwright himself.

In the decor of his production Planchon displayed some arresting iconography: large reproductions of seventeenth-century religious paintings depicting ambiguous states of agony and ecstasy (religion and lust), a statue of a dejected Christ and one of an exultant Louis XIV, all this to recall the historical and political ambience in France at the time of *Tartuffe*.

These elements of theatricality were particularly helpful for a clearer understanding of the complex denouement of the play. Traditionally, the resolution follows its course unproblematically, with the classic *deus ex machina* descending from out of the blue, bringing the required, albeit arbitrary, happy-end. But even if spectators understand the long tradition of comedy that allows such a thing, other important specifics of the resolution elude them. Who, for example, is the key figure "L'Exempt", and why his "Gardes?" While the latter term is somewhat recognizable, the other is baffling even to contemporary French spectators. Small dictionaries do not list the word "exempt" and larger ones are not helpful in defining the specific function of that office. Planchon's production does. Here, at the end of the story, Tartuffe is dispossessed of his liberty, a gesture that closes the family anecdote which has been the core of the story. But, that Orgon is allowed to repossess the family fortune and his honor – he is vindicated in the matter of the alleged conspiracy during the Fronde – this final act of repossession goes well beyond the anecdote played out in the previous four acts. The grand gesture of liberation and atonement is accomplished by the quasi-divine intervention of the omnscient "Sire le Roi" who has known all along of Tartuffe's criminal past and intercedes to arrest the culprit and dispense justice to all. Thus Planchon has "l'Exempt" and his "Gardes" arrive in costumes that display their true identity and comport themselves in ways that flaunt their authority: they are the Chief of the Secret Police and his uniformed police assistants: "le Super Flic et ses petits flics", the Super Cop and his little coppers. Of course what is resolved by this dramatic and brutal police action is Tartuffe's criminality which is revealed only now and was never a problematic of the play. What is, Tartuffe's immorality, his hypocrisy, lubricity and boorishness, these are conflicts no stage play would ever resolve. So the real *coup de théâtre* at the play's end is the subtle slippage from the protagonist's impenetrable immorality to his more banal criminality, a problem which can be settled by the arrest in the conventionally comic denouement. Planchon's stage writing for this production of *Tartuffe* makes the complex ending more convincing and satisfying, and provides invaluable help in dealing effectively today with this important work from another time and place.

These provocative contemporary stagings of classical French plays provide a continuous impetus for re-viewing, re-imagining, and re-presenting today these great works from over three-hundred years ago. Along with studies like Jan Kott's *Shakespeare our Contemporary* and especially Paul Bénichou's *Morales du grand siècle* for the ideological underpinning of seventeenth-century French letters, stage directors in post-war France have been in the forefront of the important reappropriation of the classics for our time. Making not only Shakespeare our contemporary but all the great authors from the past is not only an engaging challenge but an ongoing obligation. Roger Planchon reminded us recently why this is essential. "Presque toutes les oeuvres sombrent dans le néant. Celles qui demeurent deviennent 'les classiques'. Solides et rasurrants piliers de notre Culture. Mais peut-être les classiques ont-ils une fonction plus secrète ... A travers les gardiens de musée (les régisseurs), une époque met en scène ce qu'elle comprend ... Et les piliers de notre culture ont bien une fonction secrète: nous renvoyer à nous-même et nous interroger". ["Almost all literary works fall into oblivion. Those that survive become 'classics', solid, reassuring pillars of our Culture. But perhaps the classics have a more secret function. ... Through the museum-keepers (stage directors), an era puts on stage what it understands ... and the pillars of our culture have indeed a secret function: to make us confront and question ourselves."] (Molière, 1986: 7–8).

References

Barthes, Roland (1963) *Sur Racine*. Paris: Le Seuil
Barthes, Roland (1964) *Essais critiques* Paris: Le Seuil
Biscos, Denise (1978) Antoine Vitez à la rencontre du texte. *Les Voies de la creation théâtrale*, 6, 193–277
Bradby, David (1984) *The Theatre of Roger Planchon*. Cambridge: Chadwyck-Healy
Bradby, David (1991) *Modern French Drama 1940–1990* (Revised). Cambridge: Cambridge University Press
Bradby, David and Williams, David (1988) *Directors' Theatre*. New York: St. Martin's Press, 51–83 (on Roger Planchon)
Brunet, Pierre (1967) editor *Tartuffe* dans la mise en scène de Roger Planchon. Paris: Hachette
Chéreau, Patrice (1969) "Notre dossier sur *Dom Juan*". *Approches*, 10. Lyon: Compagnie du Cothurne
Chéreau, Patrice (1969) director: *Dom Juan* (1969), Théâtre de Sartrouville, Sartrouville
Copfermann, Emile (1977) *Théâtres de Roger Planchon*. Paris: Editions 10/18
Corvin, Michel (1985) *Molière et ses metteurs en scène d'aujourdhui*. Lyon: Presses Universitaires de Lyon
Corvin, Michel (1989) "Une Ecriture plurielle." In *Le Théâtre en France*, edited by J. de Jomaron, Vol. 2, 407–450. Paris: Armand Colin
Corvin, Michel (1991) *editor Dictionnaire encyclopédique du théâtre*. Paris: Bordas
Daoust, Yvette (1981) *Roger Planchon: Director and Playwright*. New York: Cambridge University Press
Demarcy, Richard (1973) *Eléments d'une sociologie du spectacle*. Paris: Edition 10/18
Dort, Bernard (1971) *Théâtre réel*. Paris: Le Seuil
Dort, Bernard (1977) "L' Age d'or ou, la mise en scène des classiques en France entre 1945 et 1960." *Revue d'Histoire Littéraire de la France*, November–December, 1002–1015
Dort, Bernard (1979) *Théâtre en jeu*. Paris: Le Seuil
Dort, Bernard (1988) *La Représentation émancipée*. Avignon: Actes Sud, especially 171–184
Dort, Bernard (1989) "L'Age de la représentation." In *Le Théâtre en France*, edited by J. de Jomaron, vol. 2, pp. 451–534. Paris: Armand Colin
Elam, Keir (1980) *The Semiotics of Theatre and Drama*. London: Methuen
Féral, Josette (1985) editor *Théâtralité, Ecriture, et Mise en scène*. Québec: Editions Hurtubise
Geray, Christine (1974) *Dom Juan de Molière*. Paris: Hachette ("Profil d'une oeuvre" #49)
Girault, Alain (1973) "Pourquoi monter un classique?" *La Nouvelle Critique*, 69, 78–80
Jourdheuil, Jean (1970) "Que faire des classiques?" *Travail théâtral*, 1, 86–91
Kowzan, T. (1975) *Littérature et spectacle*. The Hague: Mouton
Kowzan, T. (1978) *Le Tartuffe* de Molière dans une mise en scène de Roger Planchon. *Les Voies de la création théâtrale*, 6, 279–340
Léonardini, J.-P. (1970) "La Cage à miroirs." *Travail théâtral*, 1, 83–85
Lindenberg, Daniel (1989) "Jean-Pierre Vincent à Nanterre." *Esprit*, 155, 130–132
Mambrino, Jean (1977) Entretien avec Roger Planchon. *Etudes*, 347, 217–234
Merle, André (1974) "*Tartuffe* mis en scène par Roger Planchon." *Travail théâtral*, 17, 40–45
Mignon, P.-L. (1986) *Le Théâtre au XXè Siècle*. Paris: Gallimard
Miller, J.G. (1977) *Theatre and Revolution in France since 1968*. Lexington: French Forum
Molière (1967) *Le Tartuffe*, Notes by Roger Planchon. Paris: Hachette
Molière (1986) *L'Avare*, Preface by Roger Planchon. Paris: Livre de Poche
Pavis, P. (1980) *Dictionnaire du théâtre*. Paris: Editions Sociales
Pavis, P. (1986) *Marivaux à l'épreuve de la scène*. Paris: La Sorbonne
Pavis, P. (1992) *Theatre at the Crossroads of Culture*, tr. by Loren Kruger. London: Routledge, 48–74 (classics & moderns)

Planchon, Roger (1962) director: *Tartuffe*, Théâtre de la Cité, Villeurbanne and (1973) Théâtre National Populaire, Paris

Planchon, Roger (1970) director: *Bérénice*, Théâtre Montparnasse, Paris

Planchon, Roger (1971) "Une Lettre à Richard Demarcy." *Travail théâtral*, 2, 161 (on *Bérénice*)

Planchon, Roger (1975) "Correspondance avec une spectatrice." *La Nouvelle Critique*, 85, 30–31; see also "Le Dossier Planchon", 21–29

Planchon, Roger (1986) "Roger Planchon en compagnie des poètes." *Théâtre en Europe*, 9. (See also entries under Molière)

Romero, Laurence (1974) *Molière: Traditions in Criticism*. Chapel Hill: University of North Carolina Press

Romero, Laurence (1982) "Remembrance of Things Past: French Theatre Praxis Today." *Modern Drama*, 25 (3), 387–398

Romero, Laurence (1988) "Texte classique/Contexte moderne." *Theatre and Society in French Literature. French Literature Series*, 15, 68–78

Roubine, J.-J. (1980) *Théâtre et mise en scène*. Paris: PUF

Sandier, Gilles (1970) *Théâtre et combat*. Paris: Stock, 151–196

Sandier, Gilles (1976) editor. *Dom Juan dans la mise en scène de Patrice Chéreau*. Paris: Editions de L'Avant-Scène

Sandier, Gilles (1982) *Théâtre en crise*. Grenoble: La Pensée sauvage

Simon, Alfred (1972) editor *Tartuffe dans la mise en scène de Roger Planchon*. Paris: Editions de L'Avant-Scène

Simon, Alfred (1979) *Le Théâtre à bout de souffle?* Paris: Le Seuil

Vilar, Jean (1974) *Théâtre service public*. Paris: Gallimard

Vincent, Jean-Pierre (1977) director, *Le Misanthrope*, Théâtre National de Strasbourg and (1984) Comédie française, Paris

Vitez, Antoine (1971) director, *Andromaque*, "Productions d'Aujourd'hui", Paris

Vitez, Antoine (1975) director, *Phèdre*, Théâtre des Quartiers d'Ivry, Ivry and International Theatre Festival, Avignon

Vitez, Antoine (1978) director, The Molière Cycle, Théâtre des Quartiers d'Ivry, Ivry

Vitez, Antoine (1991) *Le Théâtre des idées*. Paris: Gallimard

Vitez, Antoine and E. Copfermann (1981) *De Chaillot à Chaillot*. Paris: Hachette

Whitton, David (1987) *Stage Directors in Modern France*. Manchester: Manchester University Press, 239–255 (on Roger Planchon)

Molière's *Dom Juan* Adapted for Brecht's Berliner Ensemble

Peter W. Ferran

In keeping with Brecht's aesthetic policy of adapting world dramatic classics for his Epic Theatre, the Berliner Ensemble used its collaborative adaptation of Molière's *Dom Juan* to inaugurate its permanent home, the Theater am Schiffbauerdamm, in March, 1954. Like the other post-1950 adaptations meant for the permanent repertory of this new theatre company, the reworked Molière comedy exhibits Brecht's theoretical and practical theatre aims, particularly in its performance potential as a recognizably Molièresque comedy rooted in *commedia dell'arte* style and also as a Brechtian comedy defined by the gestical thrust of "the socially comic" (*das gesellschaftlich komische*). In addition to rescuing Molière's socially satirical Don Juan from subsequent theatrical tradition's romantic heroizing of him, the Brechtian version redefines the charming social parasite as both a ridiculous egoist and an example of a dangerously attractive, theatrically mythic personality type. In this, the Brechtian version recovers an essential thrust of Molière's comic intention.

KEY WORDS: Molière, Brecht, *Don Juan*, Comedy, Epic theatre, Berliner Ensemble adaptations.

The Berliner Ensemble marked its official possession of the Theater am Schiffbauerdamm on March 19, 1954, with a production of Molière's *Dom Juan*. The text was an adaptation. It was described on the *Program's* cover as follows:

DON JUAN
oder
DER STEINERNE GAST

Komödie in vier Akten von
MOLIÈRE

Bearbeitet und übersetzt von
ELISABETH HAUPTMANN
und dem

Berliner
Ensemble

Musik von
JEAN-BAPTISTE LULLY

Eingerichtet von
Paul Dessau

In addition to inaugurating the permanent home of Europe's most impressive post-war theatre company, this four-act version of Molière's comedy takes its place among the five other adaptations of European drama that Brecht made after returning to Europe in 1947: the reworking of Sophocles' *Antigone*, done in Switzerland in 1948; and then, between 1950 and 1954, Lenz's *The Tutor*, Anna Seghers's *Trial of Joan of Arc at Rouen 1431*, Shakespeare's *Coriolanus*, and Farquhar's *The Recruiting Officer*. In accord with his wishes, Brecht's editors gathered these six plays into volume six of the 1967 *Gesammelte Werke* (Frankfurt/Main: Suhrkamp Verlag), which is subtitled *Bearbeitungen*. With the exception of *Antigone*, all were worked up for performance by the Berliner Ensemble, for which reason critics have since referred to them as the *Berliner Ensemble Bearbeitungen*. (The English translation, *Bertolt Brecht: Collected Plays, Volume 9*, edited by Ralph Manheim and John Willett, omits *Antigone*.)

As a group, these collaborative reworkings have occasioned the predictable critical concerns: how to define an adaptation's "true" author; how to determine the amount of textual composition that is Brecht's own; whether to ascribe the published texts to Brecht at all.[1] The authorship question about *Don Juan* is perhaps best synopsized by Jan Knopf:

> In sum: regarding the Molière adaptation, it is a matter of a team effort by the Brecht school, using the translation of Neresheimer; Brecht's part in the work is not to be estimated as very great, even though it must be assumed that he exerted influence on it

---

[1] John Fuegi argues that most of what we now read as "Brecht's" adaptation of Molière's *Dom Juan* was contributed by translator Elisabeth Hauptmann, who used large portions of Eugen Neresheimer's German translation, and by director Benno Besson, one of Brecht's prize pupils of the mid-1950s, whose idea it originally was to adapt this play. Therefore, avers Fuegi, this adaptation, along with many other of "Brecht's plays", might more properly be labelled "of the school of Brecht". ("Whodunit", pp. 159–60.) Eric Bentley's is a simpler view: "in the text that results from collaboration what one hears is one voice, recognizable only from the other works of the one poet, Bertolt Brecht". ("The Influence of Brecht", pp. 190–91.)

and that his ideas were at the very least taken into consideration. (*Brecht-Handbuch: Theater*, p. 321. This translation and all others not specifically attributed are mine.)

But there are more important issues, stemming only partly from this question. The Brechtian team work involves not only writers, but directors and actors as well. What exactly was their contribution to the collaborative creation in question? Then: Why did Brecht and his collaborators decide to include a version of Molière's *Dom Juan* in the repertory of this new East European theatre ensemble? And then: What sort of *comedy* is it?

Because all of the Berliner Ensemble's collaborative productions – original texts and *Bearbeitungen* – carry critical implications about Brecht's dramatic output and theatre work, it is necessary to study the adaptations as "Brechtian" works. We must consider the primary critical activity regarding them to be that of *reading Brecht*. And this implies a cognizance of how Brecht's ideas about his "Epic Theatre" bear on the choice and the re-working of each play as something with a potential life in theatre performance. Furthermore, if (as seems self-evident) the Brecht team's adapting a play from another culture and time also exploits the dramatic and theatrical conventions from that other period and author, then the reading of the adaptation must also entail an estimation of the *Brechtian reading* of the original. All this is part of the collaboration which produced the adaptation in the first place.

This essay offers an evaluative interpretation of the Brecht collective's appreciation of Molière's play in its whole dramatic/theatrical nature, as that appreciation informs a completed textual work designed for performance in Brecht's theatre. The plays are compared in a practically generic way, to discover how they play and affect audiences as *comedy*. Focussing on the ways Brecht and his collaborators worked up their performable version of *Don Juan*, this analysis leads to an understanding of the play that also explains how it belongs in the early repertory of that singular theatre company established in the socialist state formerly known as the German Democratic Republic.

The Berliner Ensemble's project was to include this particular dramatic classic in its new, post-war repertory because the figure of Don Juan represented an attractive social danger. A romantic hero who privileged himself against a background of questionable social conditions, he had been fashioned essentially by dramatic and theatrical tradition, and so he was able to invade the popular imagination as an appealing, but uncriticized, phenomenon. The Brecht collective read Molière's *Dom Juan* as the seminal representation of this "mythicized" figure. Engendered in the socio-political conditions of the European Renaissance – particularly those of seventeenth-century absolutist France – and represented in a theatrical style rooted in the *commedia dell'arte* tradition, this Don Juan provided the perfect subject for the new comic mode of Epic Theatre, which rested on the Brechtian idea of "the socially comic". To refashion Molière's hero gestically so as to make him "socially comic", the Berliner Ensemble first had to rescue Don Juan from a dramatic tradition in Europe that had rendered him unaccountably heroic and dashing by turning him into various breeds of "noble individual". Second, they had to submit him to a new kind of theatrical enactment – the "Epic" methods of acting and staging. Finally, this Brechtian re-composition and re-presentation of Molière's germanely comic Don Juan would make him gestically recognizable as a socially comic figure, thus enjoyably criticizable. This was the chief project of Brecht's Epic Theatre in general.

The major criticism of this adapted *Don Juan* tends to restrict itself to substantive analysis and to the thematic and ideological conclusions which result therefrom. Commentators duly refer to the Brechtian principle of *Historisierung* to demonstrate how the play illuminates the possibility of social progress away from feudal (capitalistic) times toward the new socialist era. They repeat Brecht's variously stated aim to counteract through adaptation the damage done to classic texts over time by routine and critically lazy methods of theatre production.[2] They quote from Brecht's comments on the *Don Juan* adaptation and its production under Besson's direction, emphasizing the point that Don Juan has been too romantically interpreted since Molière's time (first as a "daemonical genius", later as an existentialist hero), rather than presented as the satirical representative of the social abuses of his age. A frequently cited passage of Brecht's is this:

> The variety of perceptions and beauties in [Molière's] works is just what allows us to derive effects from them that are in tune with our own time. The old interpretations of Molière's *Dom Juan* are more use to us than the new (which are likewise old). We get more from the satire (closer to Molière) than from the semi-tragic psychological study. We find the glamor of this parasite less interesting than the parasitic aspects of his glamor. ("Besson's Production of *Don Juan* with the Berliner Ensemble." In: *Collected Plays, Vol. 9*, 408–9.)

The major studies arrive at conflicting interpretive evaluations of the work. Early on, Reinhold Grimm argues that the Brechtian version does not fit Brecht's program for "Epic" dramatic form as much as does Molière's play. Ulrich Goldsmith, another early critic, wishes Brecht had

---

[2] Brecht's most definitive statement on this score is the short essay, "Intimidation by the Classics", included among his notes for the Berliner Ensemble's 1952 adaptation of Goethe's *Urfaust*, but not published until 1954, in *Sinn und Form*, Heft 5/6. ("Einschüchterung durch die Klassizität", *GW 17*, pp. 1275–77.)

"left Molière's play alone and written his own". (320) Peter Christian Giese, author of the most thorough German-language study, finds the Brecht version a failure in its own stated terms of making the Don Juan figure a model for topical social criticism, because it does not make this model "concrete" enough. Giese also declares the play aesthetically inferior to Brecht's other comedies (to which category it properly belongs) on account of its "sociological schematism". (156, 159) And the author of the longest study in English, Arrigo Subiotto, uses his illuminating analysis to reach a number of related findings in support of this introductory explication of all the Berliner Ensemble adaptations:

Brecht's later yardstick for gauging the significance for us of a drama from another epoch is almost exclusively based on the dialectical feed-back between the portrayal given of that epoch, the seminal ideals contained in the play, and the historical time-dimension between then and now. The social applications of this dialectic are the content and its working out is the form (2).

To appreciate the full *aesthetic* force of the Brechtian adaptation, as it proceeds from the *dramatic work of art* that is Molière's *Dom Juan*, we must analyze its performance dramaturgy, the concretization of its comic-critical interpretation by the Berliner Ensemble. An indispensable source of information for such an analysis is Berlin's *Bertolt-Brecht-Archiv* (*BBA*), which contains several kinds of documentary material. Of chief interest to us is a transcript of a long dramaturgical discussion, held on 23 September 1953 among several of the actors, the director Benno Besson, two dramaturgs, and Brecht. We shall shortly have recourse to this discussion. The next most valuable information comes from the director's notes by Benno Besson in the *Program*, and from the history of the early Berliner Ensemble. [3]

---

[3] *BBA Mappen* 1485 and 1579 contain the various notes. Five versions of the text constitute *Mappen* 627, 628, 629, 630, and 1700, the last bearing the notation, "Korrekturen Brechts." The *Programm-Heft*, copies of which were available for purchase from the souvenir book stand at the Berliner Ensemble throughout the 1960s and 1970s, constitutes *Mappe* 1092, pages 48–59. Also contained among the *BBA* materials: recorded remarks on a costume rehearsal of September 3, 1953; a dramaturg's notes on the first two preview performances in Berlin (Oct 16 and 18, 1953); the copy for the Berlin *Programm-Heft*'s notes; reviews of both the tryout production in Rostock in spring, 1952, and the Berlin production, which opened on November 16, 1953 at the Deutsches Theater, then moved to the Schiffbauerdamm for the dedication on March 19, 1954. In addition, there is a *Soufflierbuch* (prompt book) from the Rostock production and an incomplete *Modellbuch* – a collection of definitive production photographs – for the Berlin production. Brecht's own published remarks on the play are to be found in *GW 17*, "Schriften zu Stücken" (Frankfurt/Main: Suhrkamp, 1967), and in the more recent *WERKE* 24, "Schriften 4" (Berlin and Frankfurt: Berliner und Frankfurter Ausgabe, 1991). The published text I refer to throughout is that in Volume 6 of the 1967 *Gesammelte Werke*.

Besson's director's notes for the Berliner Ensemble production constitute three paragraphs in the folded paper insert to the larger *Programm* booklet. They begin with this synoptic squib:

> In our comedy we show a comic Don Juan. Don Juan is often viewed as a tragic figure (as repeatedly finds expression in critiques and discussions). But Molière calls the play a comedy. He casts the hero with the experienced comedian, La Grange, player of ridiculous marquesses.

Besson goes on to explain that this "Versailles courtier in full-bottomed wig" regards himself metaphorically as "an Alexander of love" (we are here reminded that "Molière quite boldly tranfers the Spanish action to the conditions at the Court of Versailles"), but he no longer overpowers kingdoms and cities. Rather, "Don Juan conquers ladies' hearts. He collects love triumphs. A great hunter, a collector!" He is like the miser, "who collects money in a completely unproductive way, useless to himself and to others." It may disappoint some, Besson says, that this Don Juan "does not distinguish himself through surpassing erotic talent." And the fact that he does not have at his disposal "secret weapons that compel a woman's total sexual dependency" will no doubt cause dissatisfaction to "the many who spend their whole lives seeking such a thing without finding it". No, Besson concludes, "the great conqueror Don Juan distinguishes himself only by the ruthless deployment of his social status, his passion and his intellectual power in the service of his great, useless goal: the setting of records in his specialty. And that is comic".

Besson then introduces a familiar critical issue: "It is said that Don Juan is a convinced atheist and therefore cannot be presented comically. But is he so?" He questions whether Juan's "two-times-two-equals-four" can be considered a philosophically grounded creed to pose against religious Faith, as some have read it. There follows an interpretive argument about how Molière, in calling Don Juan a *libertin* who believes in nothing, is really using the question of religion to expose the depravity and mendacity of a class which legitimizes its authority by claiming a right granted by God's grace, but which does not itself believe in this God and actually scorns His moral laws. "Is Don Juan perhaps thinking of ceding the advantages of his social rank out of philosophical conviction?" Besson asks rhetorically. And he answers: *"Ganz und gar nicht"*. Moreover, "Don Juan fundamentally misses any chance to end as a tragic hero" because his fellow nobles, who in the interest of their God-graced authority cannot take the Don Juan scandal lightly, nonetheless undertake no effective action against him. "There remains only the mystical annihilation," says Besson. "In order to satisfy morality, the Commander goes into action. Thus does the comedy have its 'happy end'!"

Besson followed Molière in casting his Don Juan with one of the new company's most proven comedians, Erwin Geschonneck, who had played the hired man Matti of *Herr Puntila und Sein Knecht Matti*, the chaplain in the 1951 recasting of *Mutter Courage und Ihre Kinder*, and also Judge Adam of Kleist's *Der Zerbrochene Krug* – these being three of the most important early productions by the fledgling Berliner Ensemble.[4] For Sganarelle, Molière's own acting counterpart, Besson cast Norbert Christian, the slight, narrow-faced clown who would fill many *commedia dell'arte*-style and other low comic roles in the Berliner Ensemble's productions of the 1950s, culminating in his 1960 portrayal of Peachum in the company's first staging of *Die Dreigroschenoper*. Of all his roles during this time, the one most similar to Sganarelle was that of Sergeant Kite in *Pauken und Trompeten*, the late 1954 adaptation of Farquhar's *The Recruiting Officer*, which Benno Besson also directed.[5] The next important Ensemble directing project for the young Besson was his impressive *Der Gute Mensch von Sezuan* in 1956 (produced first in Rostock, in January, and later in the year in Berlin), with Käthe Reichel in the role of Shen Te. Reichel, the most preferred of Brecht's young actress-mistresses in the early 1950s, had already played Joan in the Seghers adaptation and Gretchen in the Ensemble's 1952 production of Goethe's *Urfaust*. In *Don Juan*, she was cast as the fishermaid Mathurine.

The Berliner Ensemble's Dramaturgical Discussion

All of these Berliner Ensemble associates, plus dramaturgs Käthe Rülicke and Hans Bunge and several other cast members, participated in the lengthy discussion of September 23, 1953, clearly presided over by Brecht, which was part of the rehearsals for the production's November opening in the Deutsches Theater. The *Aussprache* begins with a summary of the "interests" the Berliner Ensemble has in mounting Molière's *Don Juan*, a list including the following: the emergence of France as a

---

[4] After the historic first production of *Mutter Courage* on January 11, 1949, the Berliner Ensemble was officially inaugurated under this name on November 2, 1949, with the production of *Puntila*. Kleist's *Zerbrochene Krug* was first produced in January, 1952.
[5] Both of these actors had also figured significantly in Brecht's 1952 adaptation of Anna Seghers's radio play, *Der Prozess der Jeanne d'Arc zu Rouen 1431*, also directed by Besson; and they would both also play crucial roles in the large cast of Brecht's *Der Kaukasische Kreidekreis*, under his own direction in October, 1954. Geschonneck played the overthrown and beheaded Governor Abashwili, while Christian portrayed one of the comically interchangeable lawyers and Jussup, the supposedly dying peasant who is contracted in a bogus marriage to Grusche but then revives to play her tragi-comic nemesis.

unified nation during this late 17th–century period; the crumbling of the French aristocracy; the absolutism of Louis XIV, which rested on divine right; the economic pressure resulting from the opposition of bourgeoisie and aristocracy; the enslavement of the nobility at Versailles ("showered with honors and money, yes, but still enslaved"). These conditions, Besson declares, gave rise to the situation in which the French nobleman Don Juan finds himself: "he no longer has the opportunity for what satisfies the normal appetites of a nobleman: conquest". ("Die Position von Don Juan, der französischer Adliger ist, ist die, dass er nicht mehr zum Zuge kommt was die normalen Appetite eines Adligen anbetrifft: Eroberung". BBA 1485/15.)

Then it is pointed out that at this time – roughly 1650, when the arts were flowering under royal patronage in France and Molière's theatre career was getting started – Germany, by contrast, was suffering the aftermath of the Thirty Years' War: poverty, a dearth of commerce, no striving for unity, and no monarch. Brecht observes further that Germany was unlike all the other European nations, with its feuds, princes, and lack of a rising middle class. For Molière, he points out, the emergence of a middle class (the bourgeoisie) was decisive, because it made certain aristocratic habits, customs, and ideas comic. The Court attracted the bourgeoisie, who were gaining influence; this situation made the inveterate members of the nobility comic, who as courtiers received power and money but had to bow and scrape. "At the same time," Brecht remarks, "this bourgeois element was comic – these *Parvenus* [Emporkömmlinge] trying to imitate the courtiers they had displaced". Brecht's observations lead Besson to remind everyone that Molière sketched more of these kinds of character – the miser, the would-be gentleman, and so forth.

Brecht then asks: "What is comic about the Don Juan character?" ("Was ist komisch am Typ des Don Juan?") Taking his cue from Besson's citing of Molière's other created character "types", Brecht puts the Don Juan persona into the same category. Indeed, the German word *Typ* is generally used to refer to the one-of-a-kind person in our social midst who distinguishes himself by an individuality that, paradoxically, becomes "typical". The German "Der ist aber ein *Typ*!" is the equivalent of English "He's a real *character*!" This paradox of a "typifying individuality" is one of the defining elements of Brecht's Epic Theatre theory, particularly informing the notion of *Gestus* and its place in "epic playing" (*epische Spielweise*). We shall see further on how the idea of "character types", so essential to an understanding of classical forms of comedy – and thus to an appreciation of Molière's *neo-classical* comedy – not only figures in Brecht's attraction to older comedies like those of Kleist, Farquhar, and Molière for inclusion in his Berliner Ensemble repertory, but also gets modified in the process to fit his still developing theory of theatre. For now, however, we have this journal note of Brecht's, on the occasion of the successful premiere of *Herr Puntila und Sein Knecht Matti*, November 13, 1949, concerning traditional comedy's part in the early "Epic" production method:

the playing style was completely accepted by the newspapers ("if that's epic theatre, fine"). But naturally it is only so much epic theatre as can be accepted (and offered) today. Certain alienations [*Verfremdungen*] come from the arsenal of comedy, which is 2000 years old. (*Arbeitsjournal*, 912.)

Back in the discussion, Brecht's question about the comic Don Juan type gets side-tracked, as the talk turns to Molière's difficulties in writing and staging *Dom Juan* in the wake of the *Tartuffe* uproar. The group's remarks on this score demonstrate the thoroughness of their dramaturgical research, which would be incorporated into twenty or so pages of synopsized social and political background for the program booklet.[6] Their brief summary of these details here includes Molière's financial problems, his appropriating of items from the other Italianate Don Juan plays then in mode, his lacking time to write a regular five-act verse comedy, his getting help from Lully, the play's being banned as impudent ("eine Ohrfeige für den ganzen Hof"), and its transformation into a regular, neo-classically acceptable verse play by Thomas Corneille after Molière's death, which version then held the French stage until 1847. (*BBA 1485/16*.)

Then Brecht extends these historical facts into an interpretive link between the banning of *Tartuffe* and that of *Dom Juan*: "Molière couldn't resist returning to the theme of court hypocrisy again. He presented hypocrisy even more brazenly. In Molière, Don Juan behaves frankly and shamelessly; this was the reason he had been tragic to the Spaniards". Pursuing this line, Brecht re-introduces the subject of comedy.

More and more in the following centuries this Don Juan was played tragically, with increasing bourgeois influence, so that when we discussed it with foreigners (at popular theatre conferences), we encountered great astonishment at the fact that we were playing it comically. This tendency also holds for other heroes of Molière's plays, all figures who were comic. – Now, what is comic about Don Juan? Or, another question: Does one experience Geschonneck's Don Juan comically? – In my opinion, yes.

---

[6] Scholars who are interested in tracing the sources of the Berliner Ensemble's dramaturgy could do worse than compare the *Programm-Heft*'s background material with a 1952 article by Werner Kraus, "Molière und das Problem des Verstehens in der Welt des 17. Jahrhunderts," published in *Sinn und Form: Beiträge zur Literatur* IV, 4 (Berlin: Rütten & Loening, 1952). He speaks summarily of Molière as a comedian who "forces his hearers to come to laughing terms with the ongoing exposure of their innermost weaknesses." This audience, he says, was an "artificially structured society", which "always strives to anchor its consciousness in the depths of an enduring human nature". And he asks: "Had not Molière come to play this forgotten nature of theirs?" (pp. 117, 118).

Brecht's repeated provoking of the group to address the question of "the comic" about Don Juan does not produce a conclusive answer. Various replies come from the actors and dramaturgs, but Brecht responds to each with a differently aimed observation or question. For example, after an actor has observed that the situation is comic when the fishermaids fall to arguing while Don Juan "swims above it", Brecht states:

Don Juan, the great model of erotic man, has thereby become renowned. Like Faust for us Germans whenever there is striving, so it is with him whenever there is loving. So what is comic about this conception of love? (BBA 1485/17.)

And with this Brecht returns to the background material, reminding everyone of the need to establish the larger picture: the French social structure is in upheaval, and the bourgeois elements are rising and spreading their kind of understanding. "There is the old and the new. Don Juan represents the old. What is comic about the old? What could be comic in the eyes of the bourgeoisie and Molière?"

"Perhaps because he has to expend his energies in such a small area", offers the actress of the added character Angelika, daughter of the Commander. "The seriousness", says dramaturg Käthe Rülicke. Brecht fires back: "Romeo also conducts his affair with great seriousness; he isn't comic". Hans Bunge, another dramaturg, essays: "The one-time conquest; the pleasure in it". Brecht ignores this and pursues the question of the seriousness of the matter. Does it work comically? Why does it work comically here but not with Romeo? And this promising instruction about the elusive nature of the comic then prompts the actor of Don Juan, Erwin Geschonneck, to remark that Don Juan is actually a greater tragedian than comedian, because "he cannot use his strengths and abilities for great deeds, while on the other hand these [strengths and abilities] do not suffice for precisely accomplishing small deeds". Brecht synthesizes these comments by pointing to another contradiction in Don Juan's behavior: his lovemaking with the fishermaids is interrupted by external influences, but these he takes seriously.

What is most instructive about this discussion, with its constant posing of contradictions to apparent conclusions, is that it does not seem urged to settle these matters. Brecht appears quite content to keep them rattling around in the creative intellects of his co-workers while he raises further pertinent questions about the dramatic subject of Don Juan. On the next page of this transcript, he asks: "Wie ist es mit dem Untergang?". "What about the downfall?" is a translation that comes closest to capturing the natural pun that goes with *Untergang*, referring to Don Juan's destruction, which is also a literal *descent* through the stage trap, the opening into the "hell" of his damnation.

This concluding action of the play, in all of its versions since Tirso, has been one of the largest interpretive cruxes for critics, bound up as it is with the thematic question of Don Juan's "atheism", the blasphemic stance of Tirso's *Burlador* which Molière transforms into "libertinism". The Berliner Ensemble team attacks the issue by arguing whether or not this was the main point of the play in the eyes of Louis XIV's court. Brecht ingeniously guides the discussion to his conviction that the French court was not at all pious, rather the opposite: hypocritical about religion. It was not, therefore, Don Juan's atheism that outraged the courtiers, as much as the fact that his impious attitude was very much like their own. Brecht points out that the reviewers of the Rostock production, falsely assuming the class morality of Louis's court to be piety, consequently identified Don Juan's atheistic attitude as "progressive". Thus they were only perpetuating the historical tendency to regard him as a tragic individual. And that was why they, too, were dismayed at the Besson production's having fun with him.

The conversation continues in this vein for two more pages of the transcript, ending up in the agreement that Don Juan's *Untergang* cannot be played or taken seriously: first, because it is a "theatre ending" ("ein Theaterschluss," as Rülicke says); second, because it is merely a part of the Don Juan legend; and third, because if it had been presented in earnest, Molière would not have been reproached. Brecht's conclusion is that "the play cannot be a disputation about the existence of God" because the outcome would have to be an affirmation – "proof via the trapdoor, Hell". Therefore, "in Molière the conclusion was played comically". ("Das Stück kann nicht eine Auseinandersetzung sein: gibt es einen Gott. Dann würde herauskommen: jawohl. Beweis durch Versenkung, Hölle". – "Bei Molière wurde der Schluss komisch gespielt, sonst hätte man ihm keinen Vorwurf gemacht". (*BBA 1485/19*).

Along the way to this conclusion Brecht poses one of his characteristic challenges: "Here is something contradictory: a man does not believe that heaven can intervene. He is thought of as progressive. Molière doesn't believe such a thing either. But then heaven does in fact intervene. And so he has made a serious mistake". (*BBA 1485/18; 1579/08*.) This is quintessential Brecht, the devilishly delighted dialectician at his instructive game. He is displaying the technique whereby one's remarking of a contradiction will lead to the correct answer to a question. In this case, the question was "Wie ist es mit dem Untergang?" and the correct answer is that Molière had to have played it comically – played it, moreover, as a theatre joke, emphasizing the trapdoor and the stage effects of fire and smoke as obvious instruments for making the descent into Hell an artificial *Versenkung*.

From these ideas Brecht and his colleagues move to the next level of their interpretive conference. The question of seriousness stays afloat, as

Brecht remarks that Don Juan doesn't even have enough manners to believe in anything at all. This, quips Brecht, constitutes a lack of seriousness, for the later atheists were extraordinarily serious people. Therefore, he asks: "What about the style of presentation? What do we say about it? Do you have difficulties with Molière?" (*BBA 1485/20*). This leads logically into an examination of the acting. The young Käthe Reichel complains that the fishermaids say things that don't belong in a comedy. But Norbert Christian, the veteran actor of Sganarelle, utters the wisdom that, in order to get the comic effect, they must play everything with great seriousness. After reinforcing this insight with a contrastive reference to playing Lessing's *Minna von Barnhelm*, Brecht asks the company members if there are figures and scenes in *Don Juan* that do not work comically when played seriously. Ekkehard Schall cites Sganarelle's monologue, in which he argues the existence of God; this action, he claims, is comic only if exaggerated. Brecht doesn't answer this immediately, instead shooting Geschonneck the question, "Is Don Juan vain, in your opinion?" "Yes", says Geschonneck. Brecht: "If you emphasize this trait, the character won't work. It must merely be recognized that the man is vain". ("Wenn Sie diesen Zug betonen, geht die Figur kaputt. Man muss nur erkennen, der Mann ist eitel".)

And then Brecht returns to Schall's example and models a way in which it is also possible to play that scene uncomically. Although it is difficult to tell from the transcript exactly what Brecht's modelled acting is doing (he says: "All right, you're an atheist, but just let me ask you ... "), it seems clear enough that Sganarelle's monologue, which ends with him falling down dizzy from the strenuousness of its logical presentation, could also fail to play comically if an actor identified a wrong kind of seriousness for Sganarelle – that is, a *psychological* earnestness grounded in too much self-consciousness or intelligence. This seems to be Brecht's point, because it prompts Schall to expand his view, saying that Brecht's interpretation (as modelled, presumably) would only be comic "if the *Dummheit* were shown". Besson contradicts, identifying the comical thing as the fact that Sganarelle is right in his argument against Don Juan. But Brecht's instruction would seem to be that, in this case, comic acting does not consist in playing the seriousness of the character, as interpreted only from the matter of his *words*; rather, it means finding in the textual expression both the character's proximate aim and his commanding attitude, and playing *that*. What Brecht is leading his actors to grasp, in other words, is that comic portrayal, like any other type of *epische Spielweise*, is also rooted in the *Gestus* of each separate action.

This discussion, as we have followed it, moves from the subject of characters' seriousness to that of "seriousness" as a feature of the actors' playing – the German word *Ernsthaftigkeit* conveying something more technical than the psychological *Ernst*. The skein of observations allows

Brecht, then, to return to the earlier and by now commanding notion that Don Juan cannot be played as a progressive thinker, therefore that the *seriousness* they have been talking about should not be confused with genuineness, or honest sincerity, or any such approvable character trait. To Geschonneck Brecht says:

> In the long speech about God you must succeed in making your reply in this matter just as ridiculous, at the very least the reply of a dumbhead. He isn't even serious enough to think over what he's going to say. Otherwise we'll just get into the pickle of people saying to us: this progressive thinker!

Geschonneck's response tells us that he understands the complexity of the question as it relates to Don Juan's portrayal: he notes that the very next scene is the one with the beggar, where Don Juan makes a joke of the miserable occupation of begging.

And then Brecht delivers a summary statement about the brotherhood of comic writers to which Molière belongs, praising his comic technique and conceptual breadth as something to guide this present production of his *Dom Juan*.

> It is nice that these comedy writers really do retain the full contradictions and don't supply a formula that is immediately to be grasped. That makes everything come alive [*lebendig*]. He addresses himself to all sides with laughter, scorns atheists, and theists, whenever they're comic. Whenever something is comic, it is laughed at recklessly [*ohne Verantwortungsgefühl*]. That is why we don't want to make these oppositions too formulaic. The contradictions are in one way magnificent, on the other hand superficial. (BBA 1485/20)

The Brechtian *Don Juan* Performed

This dramaturgical discussion by the Berliner Ensemble has allowed us to hear theatre artists at work on the creation of this adapted comedy. Brecht emphasizes both the traditional comic incongruities and the social contradictions in the material of Molière's play. Therefore, as we heard, he recommends taking a properly complex approach to its performance interpretation, so as not to reduce the lively contradictoriness to a formula. We have also read his various remarks on the *epische Spielweise* of his early Berliner Ensemble experiments. Against this backdrop we may now investigate how the performance of the *Don Juan* adaptation combines Brechtian elements with devices from the "2000-year-old arsenal of comedy" to make this distinct new play.

We may start with the general note that the Brechtian version not only retains but also augments Molière's traditional comic features, those stock characterizations, incidents, encounters and exchanges, and set routines which have always defined comic drama and which had become even more particularized as the *lazzi* of *commedia dell'arte*. Besides exploiting the *commedia dell'arte* origination of all the dramatic figures, the Berliner Ensemble also introduced additional such masks as Doctor Marphurius and the cook Seraphine, and it expanded the number of *commedia*-style routines. This alerts us to the necessity of appreciating both the conventional dramatic import and the virtuosic performing style of such items as the master-servant exchanges, the farcical interplay among "low" characters, and the solo pieces of improvisatory nature. Then we will see that the Brechtian devices function dialectically with these traditional ones, both in the text's dramaturgy and in the "Epic" performance, to make the familiar comic features recognizable as such.

A further result is that the substantive material of the reworked play gets illuminated both as the satirically thrusting stuff of Molière and as the socially criticizable *Gehalt* of Brechtian composition. The changes that the Berliner Ensemble production makes from Molière's work are referred to in another *Programm* note as "some abridgements, repositionings, and logical extensions". As we shall see, these reinforce the altered thrust of the comedy, particularly as it is experienced in performance. This experience is essentially one of perceiving an intentionally "quotational" presentation of the defining characteristics of theatre, as if the frank repetitiousness of theatre itself were the indispensable condition for this play's working. Indeed, the idea of aristocratic life as *rehearsed playing* (French *repetition*) is the Molièresque thrust that Brecht and Company most cannily reproduced in their mid-century adaptation for audiences of Eastern and Western Europe.

For these latterday spectators, the experience begins with Hainer Hill's decor, which is designed as an artistic replication of the outward features of the Versailles Court. Brecht's notes on the production call for a setting that will imitate "Molière's original stage with its splendid perspectives, chandeliers, bare indications: the world as the grandee's ornamental fishpond". ("On the adaptation", *Collected Plays*, Vol. 9, 406. "Zur Bearbeitung", *GW 17*, 1257.) Sure enough, the *Modellbuch* shows the proscenium stage of the Schiffbauerdamm hung across with five chandeliers, bordered up and down stage left and right with tall hedgerows constructed in diminishing perspective, topped with a painted perspective sky, and backed by upstage palace grounds and courtyards approached by receding walkways. The *Modellbuch*'s photographs give the impression of an illustrated history of Louis XIV's France, at the same time looking like the period etchings in theatre history books.

In this undisguisedly *replicated* stage world, the first scene shows us the servant Sganarelle and his would-be counterpart Guzman, stableman to the abandoned Elvire. The action makes immediately clear, however, that Guzman is being dealt with ironically by Sganarelle; and so we perceive an action made partly of standard comic material – a droll lackey casts another as his momentary inferior. That Molière introduced his play's action with this conventional exposition, also featuring himself in a piece of *commedia dell'arte zanni*'s comic business, is one of the distinguishing marks of his comic imagination. More important than the exposited facts of the Don Juan story that we are joining *in medias res* is the theatrical fact of enjoying the virtuoso clown Sganarelle in our first moments. His is no simple nature, yet it is one of the most recognizable in dramatic history: he is shifty, from having to shift with circumstance; clever by instinct, but not very intelligent; endearing and charming, also venal and spiteful; and, most important, he is an inveterate player, always "on". His initial behavior, in which he expropriates the aristocracy's studied phraseology, posed stances, and ostentatious use of the indispensable snuff, may be perceived both as exaggerated self-portraiture and as imitative ridiculing of the established nobility. Indeed, this clown's histrionic action captures his essential nature in this plot: he "serves" both his master and his own nature by *acting*.

But the performance of this opening scene also signals the more complex nature of the master-slave relationship, as it will mark the audience's experience of this reworked comedy. Sganarelle, besides being appreciated for doing his familiar virtuoso turn, must also be perceived as behaviorally "quoting" his master, Don Juan. This is *gestical* action, in Brechtian terms. And it establishes the commanding point of the play – namely, that the artificial, practiced behavior of the aristocracy is *played*. The Brechtian quality of Molière's first scene, therefore, is that it introduces the audience to this play with its fabled title character by means of an imitative performance by the servant. The adaptation emphasizes this *Gestus*, so that when the famous persona himself enters the stage a few moments later (heralded by horn motifs from Lully's re-arranged music), the audience will instantly see that he also *performs himself*.

Indeed, after Don Juan's initially stychomythic exchanges with Sganarelle, he delivers his first monologue almost like an aria, as Jan Knopf observes, assuming a formal sitting pose midway through it. Knopf's point elaborates his important view that the adapted Lully music, used variously as "overture" to different parts of the action, lends the entire performance an operatic and artificial quality. (*Brecht Handbuch*, 325–26.) This underscores the gestical thrust of "performance" about the entire dramatic conception. Now, with both Don Juan and Sganarelle onstage the audience will already be "seeing complexly" (to use Brecht's earlier formulation about *The Threepenny Opera*): the artificial nobleman, already "impersonated" by Sganarelle, will henceforth have to be seen as doubly performative – he puts himself onstage and he is always to-be-imitated. It is critically significant that it was Molière who chose to make the audience's first experience of his title character an entertaining, theatrically "modelled" representation. This, it might be said, is very Brechtian. [7]

Most of the play's scenes employ the same dialectical interplay between low comic and "Epic" devices of performance, creating for the audience a disposition in which they will not respond more to one kind of stimulus than to the other, but will enjoy the pleasures of both modes, different as they may be. Another example of this is the first appearance of Charlotte and Pieter (Molière's Pierrot), which reproduces their folk-farcical dialogue and relationship almost verbatim from Molière. (In the Rostock production, their dialogue was cast in Mecklenburg dialect.) This broadly incongruous behavior, calling for the same standard playing techniques known to all folk comedy, will also deliver the familiar comic gratification. But what no doubt attracted Brecht's attention was the lengthy, awed description by Pierrot of the excesses in the nobleman's dressing habits. Although clearly meant satirically by Molière, to Brecht it was also socially gestical, offering the "Epic" feature of being a narrated attitude. Played with a characteristically simple wonder, but accompanied by the actor's conscious showing of Pierrot's trait as such, its substance will be placed at the distance which enables the spectator to hear it "strangely" (*verfremdet*). That is, the "Epic" actor's virtuosity must extend to an ability to *show* the character's defined attitude; the rendition of this particular speech should afford the audience both the pleasure of comic satire and that of critical recognition. In addition, this gestical emphasis on the fact of dressing (i.e., "costuming") also allows us to appreciate the way the Brechtian text continues the thematic motif of the aristocracy's performing itself.

When Don Juan holds his supercilious interviews with Donna Elvire and Don Luis, some of comedy's tried-and-true performance devices are at work. Molière and Brecht both follow tradition in giving Sganarelle a mimically observing presence and some biting asides to point up his master's hypocrisy. This is just one of the many scenes in which

---

[7] D.C. Potts (1973) has given Molière's *Dom Juan* a Brechtian reading which comes to conclusions that accord generally with the Berliner Ensemble's – although Potts does not analyze the Berliner Ensemble adaptation, merely citing it as "very free". But his conclusions about what is Brechtian, stemming from the kind of schematic and either-or premises often repeated about Brecht, tend to be too unspecific. For example:"... in [*Dom Juan*] Molière reacted towards the limitations of seventeenth-century classicism in just the same way as Brecht was to react to those of twentieth-century naturalism, and wrote the kind of play which, far from seeking to arouse and fulfill the spectator's habitual expectations in the theatre, deliberately sets out to 'alienate' him in the Brechtian sense, by breaking illusion, inhibiting self-identification, and making it possible for the spectator to transcend his ingrained feelings about life and become critically aware of the social significance of the events represented on the stage" (p. 62).

Sganarelle's comic virtuosity shines. His habits of carriage and stance, of gesture, posture, and mien, his repository of comic vocal pressures, intonations, and noises, of facial expressions, double-takes and other physical business – all of this constitutes the individualized expression the actor will bring to the playing of this scene, and it will affect audiences in the same ways to which they have become accustomed from experiencing a thousand dramatic clowns. Norbert Christian was praised in the Rostock performance for using his "limping, haggard appearance" to portray a "crafty rogue who nonetheless is basically good-hearted and at least periodically respects truth." (Erich Krafft, *Der Morgen* (Berlin-Ost), 30.5.1952. In Wyss, *Brecht in der Kritik*, 315–16.) And in Berlin, *Die Weltbühne*'s reviewer, Lothar Kusche, saw that Christian's Sganarelle had "a kind of resignation mixed into his wittiness, the resignation of all servants who have seen through their masters and are not quite in the position to venture anything against them". (*Die Weltbühne* IX, 16, 21 April 1954, 503.)

Rawly contrasting this experience is Don Juan's brazen indifference and casual rudeness as he "entertains" each visitor's orthodox complaints, which are accompanied by pieces of musical commentary that render them "melodramatic" (as Knopf and Kusche also mention). To maintain the comic rhythm, both texts emphasize the contrasting tones, postures, and gestures of defendant and plaintiff, but the Brechtian version also requires the actors to show their movements and stances as carefully practised. Underlying it all is the performance of Don Juan's outrageous unconcern toward those who express care for his well-being: the actor, showing this attitude as both studied and habitual, should induce some self-critical laughter from the audience, no matter how upright they consider themselves by comparison. And so we see both kinds of comic experience here: the clown's mugging commentary alongside the aristocrat's smug scornfulness of his social victims.

A closer look at some of the more modified scenes will further illustrate how the Brechtian gestical impetus both uses and complicates Molière's stock comic impulses and subtle satirical thrusts. Don Juan's simultaneous wooing of the two fishermaids (II, 5) demands adept physical comedy, wherein gestures and movement must serve the precise timing of lines delivered alternately aloud and *sotto voce*. Technically, little distinguishes the Brechtian version of this scene from Molière's; it is what ensues that makes the new version of this conventional comic routine intriguing. Instead of the interrupting entry of la Ramèe to inform Don Juan that a dozen men on horseback are after him, which prompts his suggestion to Sganarelle that they switch costumes, the adaptation brings in a wholly unexpected character, Doctor Marphurius, who proceeds to take the plot's promise of an impending attack on Don Juan into the farthest reaches of a *commedia dell'arte* scenario. In a hiliarious self-presentation, the doctor shows that his own twofold stake in the threatened violence is something markedly contradictory. Not only is he a plain mountebank in looking to gain some monetary compensation by attending to the duellists, but he is also a quite madly obsessive champion of the outdated custom. The audience should be as amused by his furiously decrying the degeneration of the elegant classical custom of duelling as they are critical of his hustler's promotion of the act.

Like his *commedia* forbear, this Dottore delivers one long comic tirade, in which he actually uses the famous Ciceronian phrase, "O tempora, o mores", and then, in a true parody of 20th–century custom, *translates it!* "Oh times, oh customs!" he exclaims. "The stab wound disappears, the bashed-in skull takes its place". ("O Zeiten, o Sitten! Die Stichwunde verschwindet, der eingeschlagene Schädel tritt an ihre Stelle".) Simultaneously we see that Don Juan, faced with this announced threat to his life, maintains his habitually mannered posing for the fisherwomen, while the manic Dottore continues in his character's wonted philosophical bombast: "A healthy but unrefined populace is setting about to force its barbaric manners upon the nation". ("Eine gesunde, aber ungebildete Bevölkerung schickt sich an, der Nation ihre barbarischen Umgangsformen aufzuzwingen".)

And so, by this dialectical juxtaposing of contradicting attitudes, the interpolated scene moves into its conventionally comic climax. The outlandish Doctor Marphurius incidentally drops the information about "these oarsmen, for instance, who escaped drowning and are making noise about some nobleman who owes them fifty-four ducats ... ". It must be made clear that it is *this* news which jolts Don Juan out of his careless wooing mannerism towards Charlotte and Mathurine and into a different, but equally typical (i.e., gestically unmistakable) attitude – that of the rationalizing coward. And while he is thus seen plotting his retreat, the Brechtian dramaturgy also makes sure that the audience will perceive two other, sharply contradicting attitudes: the now elevated fury of the zany Dottore, who wildly begs Don Juan to do the honorable thing of brutally smiting his adversaries; and the wailing supplication of the fishermaids, who plead with him to run away and save his beautiful self. Then the Brechtian text enlarges its bold artifice by having all these characters *kneel* to the ridiculous Don Juan, who finally answers, with typical aloofness:

Indeed, the sport seems too unequal. I will have nothing to do with brute force. Fate divides us. Adieu, my pretty children; I cannot refuse you anything.

(In der Tat, das Spiel scheint zu ungleich. Mit roher Gewalt will ich nichts zu tun haben. Das Schicksal trennt uns. Adieu, meine schönen Kinder, ich kann Ihnen nichts abschlagen.)

With this, the adaptation returns to Molière's impulse of switching costumes. "Sganarelle, I find myself in the position to fulfill a deep desire of yours; Sganarelle, you may put on my coat; give me your rags". ("Sganarelle, ich sehe mich in der Lage, dir einen Herzenswunsch zu erfüllen, Sganarelle, du kannst meinen Rock anziehen, gib mir deine Lumpen".) In this variation we will notice how the adaptation not only sharpens Molière's comic gesture of the cowardly nobleman's false expansiveness towards his servant, but also integrates the stock *lazzo* of switched costumes into the clarified *Gestus* of a social exploitation. And we also note how the adaptation succeeds in "correcting" Molière's putative mistake about the announced costume exchange – that is, how it repairs what a post-Realism audience of mid-century would consider a logical discrepancy in Molière's altering the costume exchange to "country dress" for Don Juan and a "doctor's" for Sganarelle. First, this costume change of Sganarelle's has been modified into an actual Dottore character and his tirade. Then, in the following scene (III, I), instead of Sganarelle attempting to prove God's existence by a rhetorical performance in the style of a *commedia dell'arte* Dottore, he enacts the same set piece as if it were a performance by a *nobleman*, whose costume he is in fact wearing. Moreover, this action is accompanied by still another *commedia* routine, displaced from Molière's Act IV and slightly altered: the servant waits upon his eating master without getting anything to eat himself – and this is further complicated by the actually reversed servant–master costuming. Because of these alterations, the modern audience must receive this scene's complicated *Gestus* – its intricate mixture of behavior, attitudes, and gestures – in a manifold way, even more complexly than they would see a "Brechtian" performance of Molière's already contradiction-filled scene.

Another remarkable action interpolated into the Berliner Ensemble version is the sequence of scenes featuring the band of oarsmen (*Ruderer*) hired as would-be assailants. First (I, 5) we see the oarsmen presented as natural hagglers for an increased "violence wage", in a socially comic routine which illuminates some familiar behavior: the assumption by all participants that this is how the game is played; the calculated demurral of Angelot to raise the price; the confederate cunning of Berthelot and Colin in this aim; and the frustration of Sganarelle in being taken at his own kind of game. All of this gestically defines the action in its social complexity, giving the audience more than a merely entertaining picture of conventional folksy clowns. At the same time, however, the fundamental appeal of the scene is that of familiar comic business.

The adaptation's next scene (I, 6) complicates Molière's comic action further, in theatrical as well as social terms, by introducing Don Juan's father – prematurely, compared with Molière – accompanied by the nobility-caricaturing horn motif. Like the earlier remonstrances of the spurned Donna Elvire, Don Luis' upbraidings here function dramatically as an interruption of the more urgent business at hand – the planning of the violent marine abduction. But the Brechtian modification upon Molière also creates a scene of multiple vision for the modern audience, who must now observe Sganarelle, the farcically beleaguered servant, ridiculously putting his oarsmen through a military drill in an upstage area while also serving his master in the downstage interview. This physically demanding playing (with all the *lazzi* derived from *commedia* that also created Goldoni's *The Servant of Two Masters*) once again puts the *zanni*'s comic virtuosity at the forefront, while it also gestically highlights Don Juan's social exploitation both of his servant and of the working-class oarsmen for egoistical purposes. We are also bidden to remark the simple enthusiasm of the oarsmen's brisk preparations for violence, juxtaposed with Don Luis' vehement expressions of outrage and his son's insouciant eating and drinking.

The Brechtian Act Four offers the most telling examples of the adaptation's "abridgements, repositionings, and logical extensions". The fourteen French scenes of Molière's last two acts are condensed into one continuous act of thirteen scenes. One of the most remarkable changes is the omission of the Apparition, replaced ("logically", it could be argued) by a triply repeated occurrence of "strange heat lightning on the horizon" ("Am Horizont ein Wetterleuchten merkwürdiger Art") – meaning a frankly contrived lighting effect on the cyclorama. An even more interpretively significant fact is that the action stays indoors at Don Juan's house. The end of the play becomes thereby an extended "domestic" scene, with a succession of visitors engaging Don Juan while he prepares himself for the visit of Angelika (another of the adaptation's interpolations, drawing on Mozart's *Don Giovanni*). Thus, the Brechtian version creates for its audience the usual feeling of expectation, but this particular sensation of dramatic expectancy rests further on a dialectic combination of stimuli: the anticipated entrance of the Commander (a part of the play's structured action and a piece of the legendary story), and the characteristically portrayed assurance of Don Juan that his newest impending conquest will certainly knock on the door at any moment.

To heighten and extend this experience, Don Juan's waiting takes on some logical features of his personality and station: he is having Sganarelle literally make him up; and he has appointed a lavish meal and has hired musicians, including a solo female singer. In this multi-levelled action we see the most essentially Brechtian modification on Molière's concluding scenes: it is an elaborate *rehearsal* by Don Juan of his projected wooing of Angelika, duly enhanced with decor and accompanied by music. To top it off, when the dire knocking signals the discrepantly perceived arrival (not the woman-to-be-seduced, but the inevitable figure of doom), the singer Belisa is cued by Don Juan to begin her performance. Therefore the entrance of the Commander's statue is accompanied by an incongruously luscious love song!

This gestical exhibition of a "play-within-play" defines Don Juan indelibly as a performing creature. It also casts the entire denouement into the mold of self-conscious theatre. One of the most consequential parts of this refashioning is that the visit from the Commander's statue is his only appearance, thus the telling one, of this final act: there is no leaving the house for that second encounter and an outdoor trip to Hell.

In Molière and Brecht alike, the legendary Commander is costumed as the statue of a Roman emperor, analogically linking him to Louis XIV himself. And so it is in true monumental fashion – the necessary fashion of the kind of theatre Brecht called "feudal" – that this absurdly enlarged and scarcely mobile figure fastens onto Don Juan's hand, utters his unimpeachable text full of religious homilies, and signals the sensational denouement we have all been awaiting. "A magnificent piece of theatre", said Lothar Kusche. "The floor opens up, and statue together with feudal marriage-swindler sink beneath sulphurous fumes and flames in the direction of Orcus". (*Die Weltbühne* [21 April 1954], 504.)

These undisguised effects were used by director Besson, observed the same reviewer of the Rostock production in 1952, "not with the force of tragedy, but with ironic pointedness". So what disappeared into the trapdoor (*Versenkung*) was not just the aristocratic lover, "but the representative of a certain social power, that of the nobility". (Kusche, *Die Weltbühne* [4 June 1952], 730.) Kusche also pointed out that this "theatrical sensation" had also contributed to the dispute about Molière's denouement, even if it had appealed as well to its own segment of the audience. That Besson, however, had turned this dazzling theatricality to critical account in both productions was not noticed by all the critics, as we may gather from Kusche's further remarks about the Berlin production of 1954:

> Besson's staging devoted great attention to this effect, and the journey to hell is both uncanny and funny. But as I was laughing, a woman sitting in front of me said huskily: "Shh! Quiet! What is there to laugh about? If you don't understand this, you should go to the movies". Supposedly she was a well-known theatre critic (504).

Whoever she was, her indignation at the irreverent spectator behind her may have caused her to miss the finishing touches that define the Berliner Ensemble's comically theatricalized interpretation. First, there is Don Juan's "vainly holding onto his hat" as he descends into the fiery stage trap (the hat, we must conclude, being drawn upward). Then the show of fire and brimstone subsides, along with the seductive singing (!). In this rhythmic pause, says the text, "several characters plunge one after another onto the stage" ("Auf die Bühne stürzen nacheinander einige Persönlichkeiten"). Like the principal figures of *The Threepenny Opera* who obligatorily gather for Macheath's execution, these "personalities" all utter their individually gestical final remarks, posed in their habitually defining attitudes. This tableau-like summing-up is a parody of classical dramatic formality in general, and of Mozart's final scene in particular; but in Epic-gestical terms it is a review of the essential roles constituting this fabulized action.

An elaboration on the final speech of Molière's Sganarelle, this adapted business also builds up a different expectation of the famous exclamation with which the renowned comedian ends his play. Indeed, this is a familiar enough utterance that one might expect the Brechtian version to exploit it for its most patent socialist meaning – namely, that Don Juan's divine come-uppance for his parasitic conduct most definitively affects his servant's wage-earning. But preventing any such tendentious conclusion as "the exploited worker gets the last outraged word" is an additional Brechtian theatrical device that complicates Sganarelle's final expression of comic virtuosity. "My wages, my wages!" he cries, his spare face crinkled up into a fine grimace. And at that moment, "down from the flyspace slowly flutters Don Juan's hat."

This is not just the oblique parody of the Voice from Heaven in *Faust, Part I* that some German critics have noticed. "Has Don Juan travelled up to heaven instead of down to hell?" asks Jan Knopf rhetorically. Well, of course not, although this little business does suggest a joke on all the post-Mozartian Don Juans who might have been claiming some holiness. Knopf, however, reads this final theatrical gesture as changing Sganarelle's lines from a cry for money into "the cry of someone cheated by heaven, of someone who mistakenly believed that his moral standards would correspond at least to an other-worldly reality". (*Brecht-Handbuch*, 325.)

But perhaps this is too serious? Clearly the down-fluttering of the nobleman's ornate hat is also a very rudimentary theatre joke, which has the effect of reducing the fabled moral momentousness of the play's ending to inconsequence. This by itself, of course, would not satisfy, any more than would the conclusion that *The Threepenny Opera*'s Finale, featuring the great-horsed royal messenger and a ponderous last chorus, travesties the swollen, moralizing endings of Wagnerian operas. But neither is Knopf's interpretation quite just. He says that because the cumulative theatricalizing of the play's action defines Don Juan's aristocracy as "literally only playing and thus really superfluous", what remains is "the reality of the servants, those who have to bear the real results and consequences of the aristocratic playings". And this leads him to conclude: "Ultimately, the play transfers this reality to the spectator, after heaven is exposed as theatre machinery". (*Brecht-Handbuch*, 326. "Diese Realität übereignet am Ende das Stück dem Zuschauer, nachdem der Himmel als Theatermaschinerie entlarvt ist".) But *this*, surely, is tendentious.

As with *The Threepenny Opera*, more than one impulse is defining the audience's experience of this deliberately theatrical ending. The self-conscious employment of absurdly sensational stage devices combines with the gestical lineup of Don Juan's victims, who will be observed exercising their clownish, expostulating gestures and then freezing (with what expressions?) when they spot the descending hat. Certainly the supposed heavenly revenge has been undercut by reminding the audience that this is a *theatre* story. But it is equally certain that this theatre story still packs something of its abiding imaginative force and therefore demands some moral attention in these contemporary circumstances. All that energy and artistry! What is it for? Theatre may point to itself as the agency of make-believe, but it is not doing so in order to represent itself as "merely" theatre. There is nothing mere about such a complex undertaking.

Theatrically Revising the Mythic Don Juan

Brecht always emphasized that it was necessary for the new theatre to show how the old theatre's falsities were perpetuated. One of the hangovers from old theatre, not yet purged from the popular imagination, was the uncritical celebration of famous personality types. Not only were "heroes" dramatically conceived as poetic extensions of "the eternally human", but they were still customarily presented onstage by artistic means that guaranteed the audience's unquestioning acceptance of them as such. Therefore it was necessary, not only to fashion dramatic characters differently, but also to enact them differently. The Brechtian theatre would go about this project by developing a new mode of dramatic composition *and* a new method of theatre presentation. But it would be crucial above all to show exactly how the older dramaturgies and theatre machineries worked upon the people's social and aesthetic sensibilities to keep them unthinkingly receptive to the old ideas and images. The work of adaptation served this aim generally; the choice of Molière's *Dom Juan* was one of several particular fulfillments of the same aim.

Brecht's theoretical goals for such a new theatre could not conceivably have been fulfilled by a dramaturgy and a performance method which served simple didactic ends – the kind so often attributed to him. In *Don Juan* we see a complicated mixture of the devices and substance belonging to traditional comedy and those that characterize a Brechtian mode of comic composition and enactment. The main figure is conceived as ridiculous, yes, but complexly so; he cannot be presented merely ridiculously, as if the audience were meant only to laugh at him. And the other personae retain their classical conventionality and its resultant appeal; they have not been re-modelled to suit modern prejudices. Because this adaptation of Molière's great comedy neither simply burlesques the famous aristocratic individual nor romanticizes the lower-class figures, it does not simply transform the original play into a Marxist lesson on social privilege. What it does, rather, is create a recognizably Molièresque comedy that is at the same time based in the particular sensibility Brecht termed "the socially comic". To produce the comic effects appropriate to this new feeling required the particular kind of theatrical performance that was gestical in its foundation: Brecht's *epische Spielweise*.

Brecht used the term "the socially comic" (*"das gesellschaftlich komische"*) to distinguish the realm of comedy in a play like his *Puntila* from the "storeroom of the eternally comic". To be sure, he said

the 'eternally comic' (the self-confidently strutting clown falls on his face) has a social element, but this has been lost, so the pratfall appears as something simply biological, as something comic for all men in all situations.

[Zwar hat auch das 'Ewig Komische' – der mit grossem Aplomb ausmarschierende Clown fällt auf die Nase – ein gesellschaftliches Element, jedoch ist dieses verloren gegangen, so dass der Clownsturz als etwas schlechthin Biologisches, als bei allen Menschen in allen Situationen Komisches erscheint.] (Brecht, "Das Gesellschaftlich Komische", included in the commentary on *Puntila* in *Theaterarbeit*, 42.)

And he gave the following example of how the socially grounded folk comedy *Puntila* both uses and goes beyond traditional comic impulses in its performance: the drunken Puntila retreats to the sauna to get sober enough to fire the workers whom he has hired unnecessarily. Brecht says: "The cowardliness of this flight into sobriety is a comic feature scarcely realizable by an actor without social understanding and socialist attitude". (*Theaterarbeit*, 42.) The *Don Juan* adaptation, as we have seen, is full of such "socially comic" actions. And the Berliner Ensemble's actors, especially Erwin Geschonneck, were amply cited as possessing the required "social understanding and socialist attitude".[8]

As for the elusive "epic playing", here is Brecht's *Arbeitsjournal* note about it, recorded on Christmas Day, 1952:

looked at matter-of-factly, what I have called epic playing is a playing in which the naturally existing contradiction between the actor and the dramatic figure finds its fully intended expression. into play comes the actor's (social) criticism of the figure, whom he of course must personify completely. the opinions, passions, experiences, interests of the

---

[8] See the tribute by Herbert Ihering, "Erwin Geschonneck", included in *Theaterarbeit* (pp. 219–21), in which Geschonneck is described as "theatre man and realist, comedian and truth-seeker". See also Peter Christian Giese for a thorough critical investigation of this concept in its relation to Marx's ideas about comedy.

figure are certainly not those of the actor; these latter also must find expression in the acting. (That always happened in a natural way, but mostly with little consciousness!)

in this as in some other matters, the entry of dialectics into theatre has caused a distinct shock even among those who have acknowledged dialectics in other fields (1001).

Difficult though it may be to describe precisely how an actor achieves such a dialectical representation of character, it is nonetheless true that the Berliner Ensemble's actors were successfully learning to do so.

In choosing Molière's play for its basic model, the Berliner Ensemble collective was selecting the most poetic and comic *Don Juan* ever composed. Moreover, the title character came ready-made as "Epic": he was both a "readable" cultural persona (a legend) and also one who rehearses an eternally immutable "action" (a myth).[9] This legendary and mythic figure was one of only two in Molière's dramatic output, the other being Amphitryon. But, unlike the classical Amphitryon, Don Juan originated in the Christian Renaissance; so, when Molière transposed him into the *political* realm of neo-classical France, he thereafter belonged definitively to the class-structured society of high-Renaissance Europe. He became a modern myth.

These attributes of Molière's Don Juan appealed especially to Brecht, who was determined to develop for his theatre a permanent repertory of particular dramatic classics, ones that would portray large figures-in-action pertinent to an old European culture undergoing a hopeful social and political renewal. Therefore he earmarked plays like Sophocles' *Antigone*, Goethe's *Urfaust*, and Shakespeare's *Coriolanus* for adaptation by the Berliner Ensemble, and he also set the company to mounting less well-known plays with mythicizable dramatic figures like Lenz's Court Tutor, Anna Seghers's St. Joan, Kleist's Mephistophelean judge Adam, and Farquhar's post-Restoration military rakes Plume and Brazen. Molière's Don Juan joined not only this company, but also that of the personae of Brecht's own plays selected for the permanent repertory – Mother Courage, Puntila, Señora Carrar, Lucullus, Azdak, and Arturo Ui. All of these were conceived as remarkable and contradictory dramatic figures intended for a mythic and legendary re-fashioning through the new artistic processes of Epic Theatre.

The Brecht collective's reading of *Dom Juan* was similar to some others at about mid-century which began to glimpse Molière's subtle satire in the performance that inhered in the dramaturgy, and not alone in the

---

[9] I am indebted to Oscar Mandel for this conceptual structure as a way both to distinguish and to fix Don Juan. See his first chapter, "The Legend of Don Juan".

text's literary features.[10] Seeing Don Juan himself as the chief exponent of that feudal social structure which still needed satirical criticism, the Brechtian version aimed also to dilute further the received image of a Romantic individual. To accomplish this, the mythic Don Juan had not only to be somewhat re-written, but also to be played in a different way than the older comedy had.

A just interpretation of the Brechtian *Don Juan* depends, therefore, on analyzing it as a "socially comic" drama to be "epically played". And the first thing to note is that the "epic playing" of the title phenomenon serves to make him transparently *fashioned*: Don Juan is being shown *as a theatrical creation*, a performed and performing persona. Furthermore, this presented persona bears the manifold marks of his fashioning and *re*-fashioning through the long dramatic and theatrical tradition that extends from pre-Molière contexts through Molière's own and beyond, into Romantic and 19th–century artistic milieux. Thus the Berliner Ensemble's *performed* adaptation of Molière's comedy also incorporated some of the historical accretions of legend and myth about the figure, making them part of his gestical entirety. This is why the new Don Juan has quoted bits of Faust and Don Giovanni about him, as well as parodied whiffs of Hoffmann's and Grabbe's early 19th–century Don Juan (the last paired with a new Faust), and of the several later Kierkegaard-inspired versions of the suffering existentialist.

And so we may appreciate how the 1953–54 Berlin audience's theatre experience should have consisted in an enjoyment of the process of *critically* observing a gestically complex social phenomenon, comically presented as a figure who owed his renown principally to the theatre. The purpose of making such an "historicized" presentation is that the Don Juan *Typ*, conceived and presented as "socially comic", should become *otherwise* legendary and mythic. Theatre audiences should henceforth read and know "Don Juan" as the ridiculously self-performing, habitually sensual, socially exploitative egoist. Therefore should he be recognized as one of the most dangerously entertaining types in the post-Renaissance theatre world.

---

[10] W.G. Moore's 1949 *Molière: A New Criticism* – with its revolutionary chapter on the "Stage", its warning against reading Molière's characters strictly psychologically, and its proposal of "a field of investigation as yet largely unexplored ... the aesthetic of comedy" – expanded the critical perspective and paved the way for such a recent reading of the egoistical nobleman as "a dangerous and disturbing social phenomenon" (Potts, 68), and for such a bold new interpretation as Michael K. Spingler's, which makes us see how Molière satirized his society in theatrical images and structures as well as in the more overtly literal ways explicated by many literary critics. (See Spingler's "The Àctor and the Statue: Space, Time, and Court Performance in Molière's *Dom Juan*", *Comparative Drama* 25: 351–68.)

But we must recognize this Brechtian interpretive thrust as going further, or we will simply be settling for that simplistic assessment of Brecht as Marxist propagandist. What the Berliner Ensemble's "Epic"-style performance of this adaptation of Molière's brilliant comedy meant ultimately to accomplish was the refocusing of its audiences' theatre-watching apparatus. This aim, if fulfilled, would have given the audience of post-war Europe – especially the people of the new socialist German Democratic Republic – to recognize, with the satisfaction that properly belongs to theatrical entertainment, the unsettling fact that *all* societies have the bad habit of lionizing just such flattering, privileged egoists as Don Juan. Being thrilled by the combination of their untouchable criminality, their dashing individuality, and their bold self-entitlement, people everywhere mythicize these personalities to the point where they must indeed appear to be larger-than-life beings who deserve, if not some form of worship, at least the conferral of some social or civic authority. The Don Juans of this type are still abroad, and the entertainment-hungry people are more susceptible than ever to the romanticizing power of the popular arts. Who is responsible, then, if these self-aggrandizing individualists gain the power to exercise their tyranny over us?

Brecht understood the immanent power of theatre to supply audiences the pretext for uncritically celebrating art's mythic heroes, for simply diverting themselves with history's legendary personalities. He had always determined to create a new form of theatre which would not romanticize such figures, would not present them as empathically appealing exaggerations of a supposedly fixed human nature, and would not allow them to be enjoyed inconsequentially. The new theatre which Brecht had called "Epic" all his life and then re-labelled "Dialectic" in these last Berlin years would instead dedicate itself to showing people how they could require the theatre to do something more socially productive than merely entertain them: they could have a theatre which invited them to exercise their critical disposition in the playhouse. This would be the new aesthetic pleasure appropriate to the *"wissenschaftliche Zeitalter"*, the age of applied knowledge. In such an age, a theatrical representation of the famous, socially privileged sexual conqueror Don Juan should be one that was both comic and consequential, at once artistically pleasureable and intellectually satisfying.[11]

---

[11] David Whitton's admirable survey, Molière: *Dom Juan* (Cambridge University Press, 1995) appeared while this article was in editorial preparation.

References

Bentley, Eric (1990) "The Influence of Brecht". In *Re-Interpreting Brecht*, edited by Pia Kleber and Colin Visser. Cambridge: Cambridge University Press

Brecht, Bertolt (1973) *Arbeitsjournal*. Frankfurt/Main: Suhrkamp Verlag

Brecht, Bertolt (1967) *Gesammelte Werke 6*. Frankfurt/Main: Suhrkamp Verlag

Brecht, Bertolt (1972) *Collected Plays, Volume 9*, edited by Ralph Manheim and John Willett. New York: Random House

Fuegi, John (1974) "Whodunit: 'Brecht's' Adaptation of Molière's *Don Juan*". *Comparative Literature Studies* 11: 159–172

Giese, Peter Christian (1974) *Das 'Gesellschaftlich-komische': Zu Komik und Komödie am Beispiel der Stücke und Bearbeitungen Brechts*. Stuttgart: J. B. Metzlersche Verlagsbuchhandlung

Goldsmith, Ulrich K. (1989) "Brecht as Adaptor of Molière". In *Studies in Comparison*, edited by Hazel Barnes, William M. Calder III, and Hugo Schmidt. New York: Peter Lang Publishing, Inc. (Originally published in: *Proceedings of the IVth Congress of the International Comparative Literature Association*, pp. 875–881. The Hague and Paris: Mouton and Co., 1966.)

Grimm, Reinhold (1961) *Bertolt Brecht und die Weltliteratur*. Nürnberg: Verlag Hans Carl

Howarth, W. D. (1981) *Molière: A Playwright and His Audience*. Cambridge: Cambridge University Press

Howarth, W. D. and Thomas Merlin, eds. (1973) *Molière: Stage and Study. Essays in Honour of W. G. Moore*. Oxford: Oxford University Press

Hubert, J. D. (1962) *Molière and the Comedy of Intellect*. Berkeley and Los Angeles: University of California Press

Kleber, Pia, and Colin Visser, eds. (1990) *Re-interpreting Brecht: His Influence on Contemporary Drama and Film*. Cambridge: Cambridge University Press

Knopf, Jan (1980) *Brecht-Handbuch: Theater*. Stuttgart: J. B. Metzlersche Verlagsbuchhandlung

Kusche, Lothar (1954) "Don Juan am Schiffbauerdamm", *Die Weltbühne* IX, 16 (21 April)

Kusche, Lothar (1952) "Don Juan oder Der Adel verschwand in der Versenkung", *Die Weltbühne* VII, 23 (4 June)

Mandel, Oscar (1963) *The Theatre of Don Juan. A Collection of Plays and Views, 1630–1963*. Lincoln: University of Nebraska Press

Potts, D. C. (1973) "*Dom Juan* and 'Non-Aristotelian Drama'." In *Molière: Stage and Study*, edited by Howarth and Merlin. Oxford: Oxford University Press

Subiotto, Arrigo (1975) *Bertolt Brecht's Adaptations for the Berliner Ensemble*. London: The Modern Humanities Research Association

(1952) *Theaterarbeit. 6 Aufführungen des Berliner Ensembles*. Dresden: Dresden Verlag

(1972) *Theater in der Zeitenwende: Zur Geschichte des Dramas und des Schauspieltheaters in der Deutschen Demokratischen Republik 1945–1968*. 2 Bände. Berlin: Henschelverlag

Walsh, Paul (1990) "'His Liberty in Full of Threats to all': Benno Besson's Helsinki *Hamlet* and Brecht's Dialectical Appropriation of Classic Texts". In *Re-interpreting Brecht*, edited by Kleber and Visser. Cambridge: Cambridge University Press

Wittkowski, Wolfgang (1984) "Aktualität der Historizität: Bevormundung des Publikums in Brechts Bearbeitungen". In *Brechts Dramen: Neue Interpretationen*, edited by Walter Hinderer. Stuttgart: Reclam

Wyss, Monika, ed. (1977) *Brecht in der Kritik*. München: Kindler Verlag

Changing the Limits: Molière, Planchon, and *L'Avare*

Helen L. Harrison

Molière's *L'Avare* and Roger Planchon's 1986 production of that comedy play on money's threat to aesthetic and social limits. Drawing parallel boundaries between modes of economic behavior, between social classes, and between the world of the play and that of the spectators, Molière's text depicts the theatre as a domain in which the monetary interests which afflict prosaic, daily life cannot triumph. In so doing he makes a claim for theatre's political usefulness but also points to the theatrical, and potentially false, nature of the nobility. In accentuating the spectacular side of Molière's text, Planchon transposes the problem of class boundaries in ways that undermine distinctions between art for an elite and art for the masses. Both productions exploit the audience's wish to belief in theatre's superiority to monetary influence. Both question the cultural role of the stage and debunk facile denunciations of commercialism.

KEY WORDS: Molière, Money in theatre, Planchon, Théâtre National Populaire, Theatricality.

When Roger Planchon stages a classical play, the audience expects to see a familiar text rewritten.[1] Planchon's 1986 version of Molière's *L'Avare* did not disappoint this expectation. Scenes appeared out of order, the scenery fell apart in the final act, the miser's money made Mariane hesitate between him and his son, and Harpagon, the miser himself, evoked as much pity as laughter. While Planchon's reinterpretation challenged preconceptions concerning the play, his changes worked to place the spectators in a position analogous to that of the seventeenth-century public *vis-à-vis* the original performance. Both the lavishness of the staging and the attitude of the characters toward wealth helped to transpose a problem which had already been present in Molière's 1668 production: the relationship between theatre and commerce. This relationship poses an aesthetic danger and a concomitant social threat, for it obscures limits

---

[1] On Planchon's handling of such classical texts as Racine's *Bérénice* and Molière's *George Dandin* (1958) and *Le Tartuffe* (1962 and again in 1973), see Daoust, 1981, 82–111.

between art for an elite and entertainment for the masses and lessens the distance between the perceived audiences for different types of art.

The fear of monetary influence on aesthetic limits can be found in the literature of seventeenth and twentieth century alike. Jean-Michel Guy and the other authors of a 1988 study commissioned by the French Ministry of Culture reported that

"... le théâtre n'est pas peṛu, ni par les comédiens, ni par les spectateurs comme un produit, fût-il culturel, mais comme une expérience partagée. Car la participation du public au spectacle procède d'une nécessité d'ordre esthétique et non d'une logique marchande" [... the theatre is not perceived, either by the actors or by the spectators, as a product, not even a cultural one. For the public's participation in the show proceeds from a necessity of an aesthetic order and not from market logic] (13). [2]

Some three hundred years earlier, Tallemant des Réaux, the gossipy chronicler of seventeenth-century France, and Fontenelle, the nephew of Pierre Corneille, belittled that dramatist by claiming that he only cared for applause in the form of coins (Fontenelle, [1818] 1968, 305; Tallemant, 1961, 2: 906). Actors, playwrights, and directors may hope to earn their livings from theatrical productions, but these are expected to carry a value which market exchange cannot translate. The mockery of Corneille and the protestations of Guy and his collaborators remind us that "The denial of economy and of economic interest... finds its favourite refuge in the domain of art and culture" (Bourdieu, 1991, 197). The domain of art and culture offers, on the one hand, a respite for a society in which the power of money is universally recognized. On the other hand, where other factors still pretend to carry more weight than wealth, the cultural domain can provide allies to groups which wish to denigrate money's potential to reorder the social hierarchy.

An examination of Molière's *L'Avare* in its historical context shows that the comedy forges an alliance between the theatre and the nobles who viewed themselves as the primary audience for the playwright's work.[3] Nobles, expected to spend in a conspicuous manner, to follow fashions which dictated *perruques* and lavish clothing, and to participate in the codes and ceremonies of court life, distinguished themselves as theatrical creatures, for they were constantly aware of the spectacle they created for others.[4] Exploiting the theatricality common to the aristocracy and to the stage, the play posits parallel boundaries between modes of economic behavior, between social classes, and between the

---

[2] All translations in this article are my own.
[3] The playwright on occasion ridiculed courtiers who saw themselves as the judges of theatrical worth. (See *Le Misanthrope*, III. i. 791–96). Even such mockeries testify to the nobility's view of itself as a preferred audience, however.
[4] On the theatricality of court life, see Zanger, 1990, 175.

world of the play and that of the spectators. These boundaries link aesthetic and social concerns as they protect against the disorders which arise from placing financial gain above the high quality of an artistic production or from attaching more importance to wealth than to inherited virtue. The theatre depicts itself as a domain in which the monetary interests which afflict prosaic, daily life cannot triumph. Though the seventeenth- and twentieth-century audiences construct aesthetic and class boundaries in different ways, Planchon's public may also sense that to violate them is to threaten a social hierarchy and to undermine claims to artistic disinterestedness. For the twentieth-century audience, the mark of mercenary contamination may lie in excessive display. Molière's contemporaries viewed display as a mark of noble generosity.

Contrasting modes of economic behavior suggest that the central characters of *L'Avare*, Harpagon and his children, straddle the line between the nobility and the bourgeoisie. As James F. Gaines has argued, Harpagon's offspring, Cléante and Elise, are probably noble by birth because of royal offices which have remained in the family for at least three generations (1984, 176–77). These two characters are eager to see their family assimilate and have no wish to disturb the accepted hierarchy. They strive to behave and to dress in a way that befits their rank. Consequently, Cléante's fashionable and expensive clothing rouses Harpagon's anger and causes him to exclaim, "... vous donnez furieusement dans le marquis" [... you go to far with your marquis imitations] (I. iv). Harpagon, in turn, earns a rebuke from his son when caught in usury unworthy of his "condition" (II. ii). The miser is a recalcitrant figure whose economic habits indicate an inability to adapt to his current social station. He disgraces his family as he makes their recent entry into the nobility painfully obvious.

Since Harpagon wishes to accumulate money and to safeguard the wealth he already has, he intends to find a rich spouse for his son, and has already chosen one, Seigneur Anselme, for his daughter. Though Mariane has caught the miser's own fancy, he will not wed her if she has no property. Cléante, in contrast, exhibits the liberality and apparent carelessness with money expected of nobles in pursuing his love interests.[5] The young man is himself in love with Mariane, but he intends to furnish money to her family. When she pays a visit, Cléante insists that she accept expensive refreshments and a diamond ring, much to Harpagon's distress. At the close of the play, when marriage enables the miser's children to leave their father's household and to join the family of a generous *gentilhomme*, the audience sees a victory of noble spending over bourgeois greed.

---

[5] On differences between bourgeois and noble modes of exchange see Apostolidès, 1981, 21–22, and Bénichou, 1947, 182.

The questionable nature of this victory has often been noted (Apostolidès, 1985, 160; Planchon, 1986c, 13). Yet, such vindication of spenders appears to be the culmination of a strategy which has, throughout the play, pointed to the theatre as an ally of the nobility. The comedy shows the power of theatre and of spectacle to defeat forces inimical to display. An art which invites its public to enjoy the sight and sound of what would otherwise be unseen could function as a natural enemy of a power which had to remain hidden.

Noble money indeed sought to show itself in the aristocratic "étalage de soi", or self-display, but money gained in commerce and destined to commercial use resisted inquiring eyes.[6] Such resistance depended both on taste and on prudence. Simple caution urged that those fortunate enough to possess hard currency in a time of relative scarcity protect it from possible thieves.[7] For money to achieve the triumph of modifying social structure, of assimilating a *roturier* family to the nobility, prosperity's connection with trade had to be denied. Any recently ennobled family whose members continued to engage in trade or finance needed to disguise those activities if they intended to keep their new station and the respect which accompanied it. Raw money, unsanctified by the birth and station of its holder, might still have constituted an offensive sight. Few seventeenth-century French plays show money outside of the purse or strongbox (Gerhardi, 1983, 57–62). By promising to make a spectacle of a person obsessed with money, *L'Avare* designates itself as an exemplary scene for the struggle between the hidden strength of lucre and the revelatory power of the stage.

The miser's fear of such power pervades the text. He carefully buries the *cassette* containing the payment which he has just received and goes to great lengths to practice usury without letting his prospective borrowers know his identity. He rails against the "yeux maudits", the cursed eyes, of a servant and worries that his children might have heard talk of his money (I. iii; iv). Cléante's lavish means of self-presentation and his statement that Harpagon has "assez de bien", that he is wealthy enough, cause the miser to scream murder: "... de pareils discours et les dépenses que vous faites seront cause qu'un de ces jours on me viendra chez moi couper la gorge, dans la pensée que je suis tout cousu de pistoles" [... such talk and your spending will be the reason for someone coming to the house and cutting my throat one day because they think I'm made of money] (I. iv). As Harpagon recognizes, both spending habits and words speak of wealth to the outside world. Any theatrical

---

[6] I take "étalage de soi" from Bénichou, 1947, 182.
[7] On the scarcity of precious metals in the 1660's, see Vilar, 1974, 238–239 and Dessert, 1984, 27–41.

display, whether in the household or on stage, menaces the miser's security and his ability to place his funds as he chooses without losing his rank in society.

Harpagon's fear of an audience and his aversion to display reach a climax in the fourth act. After La Flèche, Cléante's valet, has absconded with the strongbox, the miser realizes not only that someone must have seen him visit his treasure but also that a number of people are watching his discomfiture:

> Que de gens assemblés! Je ne jette des regards sur personne qui ne me donne des soupons, et tout me semble mon voleur. Eh! de quoi est-ce qu'on parle là-haut? De celui qui m'a dérobé? Quel bruit fait-on là-haut? Est-ce mon voleur qui y est? De grâce, si l'on sait des nouvelles de mon voleur, je supplie que l'on m'en dise. N'est-il point caché là parmi vous? Ils me regardent tous, et se mettent à rire. [What an assembly of people! I do not look at anyone whom I do not suspect, and everyone seems to be my thief. Eh! What are they talking about up there? Of the one who has robbed me? What's that noise they are making up there? Is it my thief who's there? For pity's sake, if anyone has any news of my thief, I beg you to tell me. Isn't he hidden there amongst you? They're all looking at me and starting to laugh] (IV. vii).

The spectators become unfriendly eyes, possible accomplices of the thief. Those who seem the most dangerous to the miser are the spectators "là-haut", in other words, those prosperous enough to obtain seats in the *loges*. While the second and third row boxes might have contained bourgeois families, the first row of the *loges* were occupied by the nobility, the segment of the audience which would have had the greatest interest in denying the power of money to govern society and to restructure a hierarchy based on birth.[8] As the miser reveals his suspicion of people who display wealth, he makes himself the common enemy of noble spenders and of the theatre. Spenders and the stage have together engineered the miser's humiliation. He can neither save himself from the plotting of his offspring nor protect himself from being held up to ridicule.

As Harpagon crosses the boundary between stage and audience, he reminds his spectators, and the readers of the printed play, of that boundary's presence. The spectators laugh not only because the miser mourns his money, but also because he breaks the convention which usually causes stage figures to ignore them. This transgression underscores that the medium which encapsulates Harpagon guarantees his defeat. Theater dooms the hidden.

It should thus be no surprise that the happy ending is highly theatrical. Elise's lover, Valère, accused of robbing the miser, defiantly places his hat on his head to show that no one present is his superior

---

[8] On seating in the theater, see Lough, 1957, 107–108.

and discloses his identity as the son of a Neapolitan nobleman, Dom Tomas d'Alburcy. The tale of the young man's misfortunes, a shipwreck, long separation from his family, etc., leads Mariane to reveal herself as Valère's sister. Seigneur Anselme then informs characters and audience that he is Dom Tomas d'Alburcy. Such recognition scenes abound in seventeenth-century theatre as well as in the theatre of Antiquity. Molière himself had made use of a similar ending in *L'Etourdi* and in *L'Ecole des femmes*, and he would again resort to this technique in *Les Fourberies de Scapin*. In *L'Avare*, however, Molière has sketched two alternative resolutions which would have depended on the characters' wits rather than on fate. The *entremetteuse* whom the miser has employed to arrange his marriage with Mariane has proposed in Act IV to invent a rich "vicomtesse" or a "marquise" who will woo Harpagon away from the young woman. The theft of the strongbox could also allow the audience to foresee a scene in which Cléante would demand that his father consent to the marriages which his children have chosen if he wishes to see his money again. (Cléante issues such an ultimatum, but Anselme's arrival has made the demand unnecessary.) Because other solutions to the lovers' dilemma have been raised, the artificiality of the recognition scene may grow more striking here than in other Molière plots.

As Molière retreats to tradition to close his play, the comedy redraws in stark colors the line which Harpagon has crossed in the previous act. The final triumph of the spenders in the play reads as theatre's victory, for the same line which protects the stage from the probabilities which govern the world outside the Palais Royal separates nobles, such as Anselme and his family, from the cares and greed of the *roturier*, or commoner.

Thus, Jean-Marie Apostolidès' observation that *L'Avare* leaves the reader/spectator with the unsettling impression that "tout aurait pu finir autrement" [... everything might have finished differently] might be modified by a concessive clause: everything might have ended differently if this were not theatre. This statement has a double edge. On the one hand, it suggests the theatre's claim to function as a protector of a political order based on expenditure. In so far as nobles triumph here, comedy displays its ability to restore and to praise a hierarchy which money gained in trade and finance might threaten. The theatre boasts of its worth as propaganda. On the other hand, as Molière first crosses the boundary between stage and audience then retreats to a comic and spectacular world, the spectators and readers may ask whether any political message contained in this text should be taken seriously. By showing the defeat of a miserly parent, the union of happy lovers, and the reunion of a long-separated family, Molière adheres to conventions which his audience expected of comedy. Yet, the play underscores the theatrical nature of such traditions. If the recognition scene reads as a flight into fantasy, the *vraisemblable* portion of the play may end with Harpagon threatening to have Valère executed as a thief and a seducer.

Were the entire spectacle at the same distance from the spectator, this suspicion might be eased. As the seventeenth-century gazetteer Charles Robinet implied, however, at least one aspect of this comedy disappointed the expectations which his contemporaries had of the theatre. Molière, in this play, had changed his voice:

> Il parle en prose, et non en Vers:
> Mais, nonobstant les Goûts divers,
> Cette Prose est si Theâtrale,
> Qu'en douceur les Vers elle égale.

[He speaks in prose and not in verse: but, diverse tastes notwithstanding, this prose is so theatrical that it equals verse in sweetness] (Robinet, 1881–99, 258). [9]

Prose was unusual for a full-length play. Molière's first biographer, Grimarest, though often undependable, may have been partially correct in attributing to prose the lukewarm reception which met the first performances of *L'Avare* ([1955] 1977, 70). For this play, verse would have been reassuring in a way that prose, the language of the everyday world, was not. Verse would have respected the self-conscious artifice which protected the theatre and the aristocracy alike. Prose menaces the line between the stage and the public as it draws Harpagon and the monetary power which he embodies closer to the audience than would alexandrines. Hence, perhaps, Robinet's haste in assuring potential spectators that this prose, too, is theatrical.

Theatricality has its pitfalls. To present a social group or practice as theatrical can result in emptying it of weight and significance. [10] The alliance of theatre, an art of display, with noble spenders, masters of self-display, carries a danger for members or would-be members of the Second Estate. As the play associates the preservation of the nobility with spectacle and with conventions which require the suspension of disbelief, the suspicion grows that expenditure and noble self-presentation are merely theatre. The differences between the noble and the commoner may depend less upon race and inherited virtue than upon the ability to adopt the outward mannerisms, the habits and gestures of the elite. Those who learn to manipulate the codes which govern the

---

[9] In 1665, Molière did use prose for *Dom Juan*. The controversy surrounding this play, however, ensured its success until the troupe withdrew it. See La Grange, 1947.

[10] Cf. Greenblatt: "Performance kills belief; or rather acknowledging theatricality kills the credibility of the supernatural" (1988, 109).

speech, dress, and spending of the nobility may disguise *roturier* origins.[11] Even those individuals whose noble status cannot be questioned may distinguish themselves chiefly by familiarity with the spectacle of court life and the ability to assume the roles which that theatre makes available to them. Just as Harpagon can always pull off his son's fashionable wig and show that, underneath, "l'on peut porter des cheveux de son cru" [one can wear homegrown hair], one might find, behind shows of generosity, the same interests which govern the bourgeois (I. iv). Rather than an indicator of inherited virtue and infinite resources, display of wealth may become an empty signifier.

The links between noble spenders and accumulators increase this likelihood. If Cléante and Elise are indeed legally noble, they probably owe their station to offices which careful accumulation of wealth has allowed their family to purchase. The play reminds us that bourgeois money makes noble spending possible: Cléante gives Mariane a diamond which belongs to Harpagon. The very scene in which Cléante reads the terms which Harpagon, unaware of the borrower's name, has dictated for a loan points to flaws in the image of a class which, because of its theoretically inexhaustible landed wealth, can afford to spend freely. As a prospective borrower, Cléante learns that he must accept a hodgepodge of the lender's belongings as the equivalent of a thousand *écus*. The list includes some items of furniture, such as a bed and a table, but also a tapestry, a lute, a game board, "fort propre à passer le temps lorsque l'on n'a que faire" [quite appropriate for passing time when one has nothing to do] and a stuffed lizard, "curiosité forte agréable pour pendre au plancher d'une chambre" [a very pleasant curiosity to hang from the ceiling of a bedroom] (II. i). Though in poor condition and dubious taste, these are discarded items of luxury and leisure. Since wealth, for the noble spender, serves to procure diversion, Harpagon offers means of diversion.

If the noble's display of luxury and readiness to indulge the arts signifies power based on property, the miser can provide such signifiers. If money is not itself wealth but instead a sign of wealth which only has value when exchanged, Cléante and the audience may indeed blame the miser for trying to prevent his money from circulating. Yet, they must acknowledge that no other material goods can rival money in its flexibility, the virtuality which allows it to refer not to one but to all possible objects of purchase.[12] Harpagon exploits the borrower's need of cash, and at the same time obliges the borrower, as well as the reader and spectator, to recognize that

---

[11] On the *honnête homme*'s manipulation of such codes, see Stanton, 1980.
[12] See Aristotle, 1982, V. v. ii, and Scipion de Gramont, 1620, 17–18. On money's virtuality see Simmel, 1978, 212.

need. Instruments for noble entertainments cannot feed Mariane and her mother. The expenditures which contribute to noble prestige cannot function properly without the gold and silver held by the usurer.

As the text shows the flaws in distinctions between classes and between modes of economic behavior, the final homage to theatrical convention and to noble values may read, paradoxically, as both too strong and too weak: too weak for the spectators to believe fully in the defeat of the power of money, but too strong for the public to forget that the theatre has, at this time, good reasons to voice a preference for expenditure over commercial exchange. On the one hand, the triumph of the young spenders could win the applause of all segments of the audience. Nobles could witness here a vindication of their own codes, while ambitious commoners might enjoy the sight of a young man of *roturier* origins who assimilates himself to the Second Estate. On the other hand, theatre itself, especially the theatre of a troupe which often performed at court, appeared at this time as a royal gift made to the public. The monarch's protection, the pensions which he promised the troupe, and the publicity deriving from court spectacles made the Paris actors figure as royal servants (Chappuzeau, 1875, 106). Their presence in the capital testifies to the king's generosity.

The view of theatre as a sign of the king's power and of the nation's prosperity gives it a value in the political economy which it cannot claim to have in the realm of trade familiar to Harpagon. The theatre's bias toward free expenditure can thus be read as an effort to assert its own worth as an effect of the king's *largesse*. If this is so, the disinterestedness of the art and the artists grows suspect. Value, whether aesthetic or political, can be transmuted into monetary value if it draws spectators to the Palais Royal or encourages the patronage of the king. Expenditure and display come to read as oblique strategies for obtaining wealth.

Theater allies itself too closely with the nobility for any doubts concerning the credibility and the extra-commercial properties of one not to affect the other. Nobility, expenditure, and theatre all belong to a world of spectacle. If this world is merely one of illusion, the suspicion lingers that bourgeois accumulation rules off-stage and behind the scenes. Any lack of ease experienced by the original audience of *L'Avare* may have resulted in part from the demystification of spending.

The boundaries menaced in Molière's text reappear in the 1986 production of the play, although Planchon and his public might view them differently. The modern public must deal not with the possibility that money may upset a hierarchy based on birth but instead with the boundaries which define a cultural elite. The boundary between theatre and the audience does not vanish, but another distinction, that between spectacle in general and Molière's theatre, a specific part of the classical patrimony, comes into play.

To surprise an audience long familiar with Molière's comedy, Planchon exaggerated the plays's transgression of the border between stage and *salle*. Michel Serrault, the actor playing Harpagon, no longer merely addressed the audience as a whole, but instead came off the stage and threatened individual spectators. At the intermission in the Paris show, Serrault as Harpagon protected himself and his house from inquiring eyes by personally drawing the curtain. The modifications and exaggerations which are the most interesting for a study of theatre and commerce, however, occurred in the final act.

Planchon has called the ending of *L'Avare* a series of miracles, and his handling of that ending emphasizes the miraculous (1986c, 13). Rather than merely have the members of Anselme's family narrate their history, Planchon's production made those events visible to the spectators and to Harpagon, the enemy of theatre. The audience saw lightening, a ship rocked by a storm, fights with pirates, and, at one point, Mariane's mother, who, laden with a backpack, crossed the stage and waved at the spectators. In playing the recognition scene in this fashion, Planchon and his actors made the extremely theatrical nature of the ending clear even to those members of the audience who might have had only a limited acquaintance with the traditions of seventeenth-century comedy. A public which was growing accustomed to a society in which all forms of popular entertainment, including music, had to have a visual as well as an aural component could still recognize the final triumph as one of spectacle over the humdrum of daily life.

This recourse to spectacle did not merely amplify Molière's text. If both Molière and Planchon suddenly appeared to reinforce a distinction between the theatre and the outside world, the boundaries were not drawn in the same place, nor were they equally firm. Although Harpagon does not belong in the adventurous world of Anselme, Molière does not physically separate him from the other characters. As the others go to find Anselme's wife, Harpagon also leaves stage in order to rejoin his money. In the 1986 production, Cléante returned the money to his father before leaving the stage. Harpagon sat alone with his wealth while the others departed. Especially since Planchon had Harpagon watch, thunderstruck, the flashbacks which explained the identity of Valère, Mariane, and Anselme, the miser figured as a helpless spectator of a happiness which he could not share.

Any parallel created here between the main character and the person in the audience contributed to making the audience accept the director's interpretation of the comedy. Planchon reads *L'Avare* as the story of a businessman who becomes a miser when he has lost all, when he realizes that he is old (1986c, 10). The audience should and does pity the miser. As most spectators expect eventually to know old age, they sympathize with Harpagon's fate.

To do so no longer presents the problems which it would have in Molière's time. Planchon did not play for an absolute monarch and his court, nor could he believe that his actors performed chiefly for an audience which would necessarily resent the power of capital. Many members of the audience might have belonged to an intellectual elite which deemed itself capable of appreciating Planchon's handling of a classic, but the casting of the popular Michel Serrault in the role of Harpagon makes any limiting identification of the audience precarious.[13] Even with Serrault as an attraction, the director could not expect that great numbers of spectators in Villeurbanne would be workers, who, he has lamented, "go into a theatre only to build them" (Daoust, 1981, 218). When the production moved to Paris and to the Mogador, a "théâtre de boulevard", the public found itself in the midst of a wealthy shopping district, near the opera and the "grands magasins" which first catered to the bourgeois of the nineteenth century. The power of capital might have been more tangible in this private theatre than in either Villeurbanne or a Parisian national theatre, such as the Théâtre de la Porte Saint-Martin, which Planchon had used for the May 1974 production of *Le Tartuffe* (Planchon, 1974). Whatever the spectators' reasons for seeing *L'Avare*, they were people with time and money to spend on the theatre and people who witnessed in that same year the return of the right and of pro-business forces to power as Jacques Chirac became prime minister. Foolish as it would be to assume that all the spectators were wealthy or were supporters of Chirac's government, they were accustomed to the idea of money's ability to structure society. As a representative of a social force, Harpagon had triumphed long ago.

Planchon's reinterpretation did not deny the threat of money, but instead displaced it. Money still menaced personal happiness. Mariane, who throughout this production had hesitated between Harpagon's wealth and Cléante's youth, returned to the stage at the end and gave her rejected suitor a parting glance which reduced him to tears. The tenuous happy ending could thus be undermined by the greed of the young as well as by that of the old. A troubling aspect of money lay, once again, in its relation to theatrics.

The spectacle at the end of *L'Avare* reminded the audience that money can usually only be defeated with money. This was already apparent in Molière's text. Anselme could free the young lovers' from Harpagon's wealth because he was not only noble but also rich. With his no doubt expensive machines, Planchon made the audience see the monetary force which allowed spectacle to bring the threat of the miser under control.

---

[13] While it is impossible to verify Cournot's assertion that Serrault was chiefly responsible for the financial success of the production, it seems probable that this actor drew crowds.

Expenditure of money might replace the hoarding of money as a victorious economic mode, but the financial side of the triumph became more visible than in Molière's production.

This financial side involves not only the means of theatrical production but also the possible gains which it evokes. In watching the lavish staging of *L'Avare*, the audience saw techniques recalling performance genres which are generally more lucrative than the classical theatre. One reviewer, Guy Dumur, found that Planchon's imaginative creations in this play would have been better suited to some romantic melodrama than to Molière's text (1986, 105). The flashbacks of the final act may have reminded the audience of cinema. The presence of performers, such as Michel Serrault and Annie Girardot, who owed their reputation to the screen rather than to the stage, reinforced this second association, as did what Michel Cournot called the "mégalomanie hollywoodienne" which caused Planchon to use an elaborate set and to show, in great detail, the daily life in and around the miser's house. Planchon appeared to overstep the boundaries which define classical theatre and to verge into borrowings from other media.

The triumph of theatre and of comic tradition gave way here to a triumph of spectacle. This might have suited Planchon's view of the all-encompassing role of the theatre as an institution. Planchon refuses to confuse media and to allow, for instance, the videotaping of stage performances, but he envisages the theatre as a place of production which would create play, film, and televised versions from one basic project (Planchon, 1986b, 26–27). The evocation of film techniques as well as the use of film stars reads as symptomatic of this wish to break down barriers between performance media. Yvette Daoust may, moreover, be correct in suggesting that much of Planchon's experimentation in the theatre derives from an effort to attract a public which is more accustomed to the cinema than the stage (1981, 8). Despite Planchon's own fears that only a radical change in civilization can bridge the cultural gap which keeps theatre from ever being truly "populaire", the techniques and casting seen in *L'Avare* do conform to the mission of the Théâtre National Populaire (TNP).[14] The TNP strives to make productions of high quality accessible to a large public, and, while film and television can reach beyond the spatial confines of one theatre, the presence of actors and actresses familiar from the screen may draw new spectators to a show. The missionary role of this popular theatre dictates that it go in search of its audience.

---

[14] On the TNP's search for a public, see Corvin, 1987, 181–21. For Planchon's fear that only a cultural revolution will bridge the gap which keeps workers from the theater, see Planchon, 1974.

Especially when a TNP production reappears in non-subsidized theatre like the Mogador, the audience may remember that to seek a public is, inevitably, to seek a public's money. Obvious and harmless as this admission may appear, both theatre professionals and theatre-goers in France balk at it. To quote again from the study cited at the beginning of this essay, "... le théâtre ne peut pas moralement se vendre" [... the theatre cannot morally sell itself] (Guy et al., 1988, 15). Hence the wish expressed by the current and potential spectators responding to the Ministry of Culture poll to see sober advertisements for theatre, announcements which provide information about upcoming spectacles but which do not appear to peddle a product.[15] These spectators, the information directors of the nine French theatres studied, and the authors of the study evince a determination to dissociate the stage from the commercial world, which has, they feel, invaded the cinema: "A l'inverse du cinéma, dont on aime à le démarquer précisément sur ces questions, il [le théâtre] apparaît ainsi plutôt préservé des logiques traditionnelles de marché" [Unlike cinema, from which one likes to differentiate it precisely in these matters, it [the theatre] thus appears rather protected from the traditional logic of the market place] (Guy et al., 1988, 145). The authors of *La Rhétorique publicitaire du théâtre* and the people whom they have questioned may be quite sincere in attributing a loftier purpose than economic profit to art. Yet, the persistence with which they refuse to acknowledge the economic aspects of theatre's success or failure does suggest that money has not lost all its scandalous aspects in the past three hundred years and that the producers of art works meant to be widely accessible still fear to hear their work accused of being commercial.

Even while hoping that an artist or group of artists will succeed, an admirer may show reluctance to associate success with money. To work for money may mean making concessions to a large public which many may view as less cultivated than that which normally fills a theatre presenting classics. On the one hand, a public may fear to see the object of its admiration degraded by such concessions. On the other hand, spectators may, on some level, not wish to be too numerous. If the

---

[15] Guy and collaborators met in March of 1987 with three groups. One consisted of ten "aficionados" of theater. This group was diverse in age, sex, social and professional status, and its members attended different sorts of theater, private and public. A second group of nine people was equally diverse but did not privilege the theater over other entertainments. The final group consisted of eight volunteers who, in schools, universities, or work places, distributed information on theater and organized outings to the theater. After initial discussions with these groups, the authors sent questionnaires to people of different ages and professions. Of the 311 respondents, forty-seven per cent had little familiarity with the theater while the others were nearer to being connoisseurs. All had similar reactions to theater publicity (1988, 23–27; 36).

authors of *La Rhétorique publicitaire du théâtre* correctly state that the audience enjoys theatre as a shared experience, it is perhaps worth remembering that that experience usually takes place in an enclosed space which may stand in opposition to the outside world (Guy et al., 1988, 13). The pleasure of the group has exclusive overtones. Members, whether spectators with subscriptions, individuals who pride themselves on their knowledge of a given play, or even spectators who congratulate themselves on their ability to appreciate the direction of a Planchon, may enjoy their status as the fortunate few. A considerable segment of the audience may resemble Harpagon in its miserliness, its wish to conserve, reasonably or not, what it regards as its own property. Though itself cultural instead of monetary, this miserliness here finds itself menaced by the image of art's financial gain.

Rather than the reinforcement of a social elite, the audience witnessed in Planchon's play the questioning of any restrictive aesthetic which would maintain boundaries between popular art and art produced for a cultivated minority. These boundaries might separate melodrama from classical comedy, cinema from theatre, efforts to gain funds from pure artistic ambition, or an audience which pays to see Serrault from spectators who admire Molière or Planchon. All such categorizations remain, however, unclear and subject to change. As the flashbacks which now safeguard the happy ending remind us, adventure, mechanical and improbable endings, or, as Planchon says, miracles, have their place in treasured literary texts as well as in the action-packed films which bring enormous receipts at the box office. The traits, such as courage, invincibility, and disinterestedness, which such films attribute to their heroes belong to the noble protagonists of classical dramas. Should these links discomfort the spectator, he or she cannot dismiss them by saying that the value scales which a small elite pretended to protect under the Ancien Régime are anachronistic or unworthy of attention in a democratic society. The urge to retain control, to protect one's cultural property from the contamination of the crowd may have various justifications, but belief in rule by the people is not one of them.

Paradoxically, lack of ease with the evocation of financial gain in the performance arts might derive not from wealth's ability to create social differences, but instead from money's power as an equalizer.[16] It not only assigns comparable value to diverse products but can also make goods and services within a given category resemble each other. Seeking financial gain can lead producers to follow set formulas, to provide the public with what it has purchased in the past and is likely to buy again. Yet, a wish to support diversity in the market should not lead us to

---

[16] See Aristotle, 1982, V. v. 14–15 and Marx, 1978, 64–65.

forget that money also effaces differences among its users. When all people able to pay the market price for a product or service have access to it, the wealthy certainly enjoy advantages over the poor, but distinctions which other societies might have used in distributing goods or in determining admission to various institutions grow less visible. With money as a common enemy, privileges based on ancestry and those associated with education become analogous.

If Molière made the gesture of allying theatre with a political elite. Planchon refuses to accept the alliance with a cultural elite. The result of this refusal is, in some respects, similar to that obtained by showing the theatrical nature of nobility. Boundaries between an elite and the masses become questionable, as do the limits which separate theatre from the commercial world. Equating financial and artistic success may be a danger to be eschewed, but so is any tendency to dismiss art which earns money. Any theatre which strives to be *populaire* will run the risk of being seen as commercial. Planchon reminds the audience that, for better or for worse, money influences assessment of theatrical success.

Planchon's performance does not dictate new limits for the classical theatre. Instead, the 1986 *L'Avare* indicates to its spectators the limits which they and their predecessors have drawn. Planchon reminds his spectators that no one owns Molière, France's cultural heritage, or the theatre. The theatre itself cannot, at the expense of other performance media, hold a monopoly on cultural value. The temptation to define that value in monetary terms cannot be exorcised by simple denunciations of commercialism.

References

Apostolidès, Jean-Marie (1985) *Le Prince sacrifié: théâtre et politique au temps de Louis XIV.* Paris: Minuit

Apostolidès, Jean-Marie (1981) *Le Roi-machine: spectacle et politique au temps de Louis XIV.* Paris: Minuit

Aristotle (1982) *The Nicomachean Ethics.* Trans. H. Rackham. Cambridge: Harvard University Press; London: William Heineman LTD

Bénichou, Paul (1941) *Morales du Grand Siècle.* Paris: Gallimard

Bourdieu, Pierre (1991) *Outline of a Theory of Practice.* Trans. Richard Nice. Cambridge: Cambridge University Press

Chappuzeau, Samuel (1875) *Le Théâtre français.* Ed. George Monval. Paris

Corvin, Michel (1987) *Le Théâtre nouveau en France.* Paris: PUF

Cournot, Michel (1986) "Michel Serrault dans *L'Avare*". *Le Monde.* 25 October, 26

Daoust, Yvette (1981) *Roger Planchon: Director and Playwright.* Cambridge: Cambridge University Press

Dessert, Daniel (1984) *Argent, pouvoir et société au Grand Siècle.* Paris: Fayard

Dumur, Guy (1986) "Molière entre Serrualt et Planchon". *Nouvel Observateur.* 23 March, 104–05

Fontenelle, Bernard Le Bovier de [1818] (1968) *Vie de Corneille. OEuvres complètes de Fontenelle.* Ed. G. B. Depping. Vol. 2. Geneva: Slatkine. 332–50. 3 vols

Gaines, James F. (1984) *Social Structures in Molière's Theater*. Columbus: Ohio State University Press
Gerhardi, Gerhard (1983) *Geld und Gesellschaft im Theater des Ancien Régime*. Heidelberg: Universitätsverlag
Gramont, Scipion de (1620) *Le Denier royal*. Paris
Greenblatt, Stephen (1988) *Shakespearean Negotiations: the Circulation of Social Energy in Renaissance England*. Berkeley: University of California Press
Grimarest [Jean-Léonor le Gallois, sieur de] [1955] (1977) *La Vie de Monsieur Molière*. Ed. Georges Mongrédien. Paris: Michel Brient
Guy, Jean Michel et al. (1988) *La Rhétorique publicitaire du théâtre*. La Documentation française
La Grange, Charles de (1947) *Le Registre de La Grange, 1659–1685*. Ed. Bert Edward Young and Grace Philpott Young. Paris: Droz
Lough, John (1957) *Paris Theater Audiences in the Seventeenth and Eighteenth Centuries*. London: Oxford University Press
Marx, Karl (1970) *A Contribution to the Critique of Political Economy*. Ed. Maurice Dobb. New York: International Publishers
Molière [Jean-Baptiste Poquelin] (1971) *L'Avare. OEuvres complètes*. Ed. Georges Couton. Bibliothèque de la Pléiade. Vol. 2. Paris: Gallimard. 507–582. 2 vols
Molière [Jean-Baptiste Poquelin] *Le Bourgeois gentilhomme. OEuvres complètes*. Vol. 2. 695–787
Molière [Jean-Baptiste Poquelin] *Le Misanthrope. OEuvres complètes*. Vol. 2. 123–218
Planchon, Roger, dir. (1986a) *L'Avare*. By Molière. With Michel Serrault and Annie Girardot. TNP-Villeurbanne, Villeurbanne. 3 March to 5 April 1986: Théâtre Mogador, Paris. 16 October 1986 to 8 February 1987
Planchon, Roger (1986b) "Planchon manifeste". Interview with Jean-Pierre Thibardot. *Libération*. 3 April, 26, 27
Planchon, Roger (1986c) Preface of *L'Avare* by Molière. Paris: Livre de Poche
Planchon, Roger (1974) "Territoire de Roger Planchon". Interview with Yvonne Baby. *Le Monde*. 2 May, 19
Robinet, Charles (1881–99) *Lettres en vers à Madame et à Monsieur*. Vol. 3 of *Les Continuateurs de Loret. Lettres en vers de La Gravette de Mayolas, Robinet, Boursault, Perdou de Subligny et autres*. Publiées par le baron James de Rothschild et Emile Picot. Paris: Morgand. 4 vols
Simmel, George (1978) *The Philosophy of Money*. Trans. Tom Bottomore and David Frisby. London: Routledge and Kegan Paul
Stanton, Domna (1980) *The Aristocrat as Art: A Study of the Honnête Homme and the Dandy in Seventeenth- and Nineteenth-Century French Literature*. New York: Columbia University Press
Tallemant des Réaux, Gédéon (1961) *Historiettes*. Ed. Antoine Adam. Vol. 2. Bibliothèque de la Pléiade. Paris: Gallimard. 2 vols
Vilar, Pierre (1974) *Or et monnaie dans l'histoire*. Paris: Flammarion
Zanger, Abby E. (1990) "The Spectacular Gift: Rewriting the Royal Scenario in Molière's *Les Amants magnifiques*". *Romanic Review*. 81: 173–88

Getting Down to Business in Molière's *Le Bourgeois Gentilhomme*

Philip R. Berk

Molière's comedy, *Le Bourgeois gentilhomme*, is remarkable for a court entertainment, one performed for the first time in the aristocratic isolation of Louis XIV's château at Chambord, in that it refuses to elide or supress questions of work and its monetary rewards even though anxious attempts for social and political reasons are made to conceal these abiding presences, which include, of course, the effort involved in the arts, and its remuneration. From beginning to end in *Le Bourgeois gentilhomme*, Molière unveils for us the artistic, social, financial and political conventions that art and society would seemingly prefer to conceal. The title of the comedy, normally understood as a monstrous collocation of a comically impossible social reality in fact nicely expresses these tensions of a reality of work and effort continuously suppressed by an official politics of courtly and aristocratic culture and of course by those who subscribe to that politics. The final balletic spectacle is ambiguously both the fictional ballet within the comedy and the royal diversion outside the comedy the invitation to which allows the Jourdains to transcend their social limitations by participating in the king's cultural monopoly on social representations.

KEY WORDS: Comedy, Molière, Louis XIV, *Le Bourgeois gentilhomme*, Representation of work, Money.

The question has been recently raised by Harmut Stenzel (1991), and answered in the negative, whether Molière's *comédie-ballets* and particularly *Le Bourgeois gentilhomme* suspend the project of social criticism undertaken in the great early comedies as exemplified by *Tartuffe* and *Le Misanthrope*. I believe that a case can be made for the seriousness of Molière's social and, particularly, artistic self-consciousness in *Le Bourgeois gentilhomme*. Remarkable for a court entertainment, one performed for the first time in the aristocratic isolation of the château at Chambord, Molière's comedy refuses to elide or supress the question of work and its monetary rewards even though anxious attempts for social and political reasons to are made to conceal these abiding presences, which include, of course, the effort involved in the arts, and its remuneration.

From beginning to end in *Le Bourgeois gentilhomme*, Molière unveils for us the social, artistic, financial and political conventions of representation that society would prefer to conceal. The title of the comedy, normally understood as a monstrous collocation of a comically impossible social reality in fact nicely expresses these tensions of a reality of work and effort continuously suppressed by an official politics of courtly and aristocratic culture and of course by those who subscribe to that politics.

Molière himself wastes no time in getting down to business. As if running counterpoint to Lully's stately overture – and one must hear this overture, now facilitated by phonograph recordings of the comedy – as one visualizes the opening scene as described in the stage directions – Molière's opening tableau is that of an apprentice musician busy scribbling a musical score: "L'ouverture se fait par un grand assemblage d'instruments; et dans le milieu du théâtre on voit un élève du Maître de musique, qui compose sur une table un air que le Bourgeois a demandé pour une sérénade". (The Overture is performed by a full concert of instruments, and in the center of the stage there is an apprentice of the music master, who is at a desk writing a melody that M. Joudain has requested for a serenade.)[1] While Lully's music is actually playing, manifesting itself as an invitation to courtly entertainment, "music" is scenically represented as a *métier* (with its institutional structures of training and certification soon to be exposed) and as work, a product of human industry that seeks patronage and requires monetary compensation. No matter how perfectly realized in Lully's score, music, most etherial of the arts, the most transparent and disembodied, is at once demystified of its "divine" status. By this initial display of work and unreadiness, a literal impromptu, *Le Bourgeois gentilhomme* looks back to the artful theatrical self-unmasking of *la Troupe de Monsieur* in *L'Impromptu de Versailles* (1663). Although the representation of music-as-work may be taken as a synecdoche for any or all of the arts, perhaps it reflects the special case, if not a special burgeoning animus, against the other Jean-Baptiste, the "divin Lully", increasingly become Molière's rival for the patronage of court spectacle.

Vis-à-vis the elaborate concluding "Ballet des Nations", the entire *Bourgeois gentilhomme* can be viewed as a rehearsal, prelude or an impromptu, a getting ready for the finished product of the final *divertissement*.[2] Such appears to be the subordinate status of Molière's comedy

---

[1] Molière, *Oeuvres complètes*, éd. Georges Couton (Paris: Gallimard, 1971), vol. II p. 711. All quotations from Molière will be taken from this edition. All translations are my own.
[2] So Jules Brody, "Esthétique et société chez Molière", in *Dramaturgie et Société: Rapports entre l'oeuvre théâtrale, son interprétation et son public au XVIIe et au XVIIIe siècle.*, ed. Jean Jacquot (Paris: CNRS, 1968), 314.

not just to the ballet, but to the music and scenery as well in the contemporary report of *La Gazette* (October 18, 1670):

> Leurs Majestés ... eurent pour la première fois <leur divertissement> d'un ballet de six entrées, accompagné de comédie, dont l'ouverture se fit par une merveilleuse symphonie, suivie d'un dialogue en musique des plus agréables, la décoration du théâtre et le reste ayant toute la magnificence accoutumée dans les divertissements de cette cour.
>
> (Their Majesties ... had for the first time <their diversion> of a ballet with six entries, accompanied by a comedy, whose overture was performed by a marvellous symphony, followed by a dialogue in music of the pleasantest sort, the theatrical decoration and everything else having all the magnificience customarily found in the diversions of this court.)[3]

To give some sense of temporal perspective, in the Gustav Leonhardt recording (1988) of *Le Bourgeois gentilhomme* (Harmonia Mundi 77059-2-RG), Lully's music for just the concluding ballet is 41 minutes in duration as opposed to 43 minutes for all the music of the rest of the work. Rather than reject such a subordinate status, Molière seems to have thrived on the marginalization, if only to give himself space to comment on and undermine the illusion of artistic hierarchization. As if imitating the leisurely pace of Lully's music, Molière deliberately retards the forward drive of the action to intall a series of nested overtures and prologues. If the *Bourgeois gentilhomme* as a whole is a prologue to the "Ballet des Nations" then the first two acts of the comedy can be seen as a prologue or set of prologues to the comic intrigue of the last three acts, metaphorical antechambers to the more public family drama that begins with the Third Act, itself prelude to the concluding *divertissement*. For in relation to the prologue of M. Jourdain's "lessons" one has to think that the first scene between the dancing and music masters itself constitutes a smaller, initial thematic, self-conscious preface to M. Jourdain's own impromptu, his patent unreadiness to become the *homme de qualité* of which he dreams. Schematically, the rehearsal-performance structure is as follows: (Lully's overture + tableau of the musician) > (Debate between the music and dancing masters) > (M. Jourdain's lessons) > (Acts III–V) > (Ballet des Nations).

The initial debate between the music and dancing masters about the relative value of taste and money within the system of patronage in which they are bound echoes by its position the moral debates that begin most of Molière's major comedies from *L'ecole des maris* through *Le Misanthrope*. The question of taste vs. financial support foregrounds the role of money as the embarrassing, but necessary underpinning of the arts – the realistic, even comic plural is important here – even though

---

[3] Quoted in Despois et Mesnard, *Oeuvres de Molière* (Paris: Hachette, 1883), t. 8, pp. 4–5.

the claim is made that artists themselves take greater pleasure in the comprehension and appreciation of their craft. The music master, in what is perhaps another dig at the rapacious Lully, is somewhat more cynical than his colleague:

Il n'y a rien assurément qui chatouille davantage que les applaudissements que vous dites. Mais cet encens ne fait pas vivre; des louanges toutes pures ne mettent point un homme à son aise: il y faut mêler du solide; et la meilleure façon de louer, c'est de louer avec les mains.
(There is nothing assuredly which tickles more than the applause you mention. But you cannot live off flattery; praise alone cannot make life comfortable: you have to add something tangible; and the best way to applaud is to hand over some money.) (I,1)

For these issues to be raised at the outset of a royal *divertissement* effectively undercuts whatever claims of transparency, magical illusion, social exclusivity or aesthetic escapism that underlay the appeal of royal spectacle, so brilliantly analyzed by Jean-Marie Apostolidès (1981). If artists demand to be paid for their work, the payment of such money requires involvement in business or taxation on the part of the producers. Neither on the scale of the production of *Le Bourgeois gentilhomme* at Chambord and later at Saint-Germain, nor within the fiction of the comedy can king, gentleman courtier, or artist do without the merchant class, even if that requires that, defensively, the bourgeois be diminished by metonymic identification with his money, as he is by the music master: "ce nous est une douce rente que ce M. Jourdain". (This M. Jourdain is a tidy income for us.) Implicitly, the arts themselves take on the problematic social status of the "bourgeois gentilhomme", a paradoxical entity that has none of the reassuring distance and analytic clarity of Boileau's phrase often used to identify seventeenth-century theatrical spectatorship, "la cour et la ville" (the court and the town).

The *paragone* or comparison among the arts has a noble history, but in the antecameral atmosphere of *Le Bourgeois gentilhomme* the debates between music and dancing master, master at arms vs. the arts, philosophy vs. arms, take on an edge of pure self-interestedness in the zero-sum competition for the resources of M. Jourdain's purse. Paradoxically, M. Jourdain himself is sublimely uninterested in such hierarchical, cultural jockeying, since, for him, the arts are not ends to be pursued for themselves, but only a means to his social advancement. The lessons during which nothing is learned, given in exchange for Jourdain's payment, are shown as hardly anything more than business transactions. The "disinterestedness" of the liberal and martial arts is dispelled not merely by the demonstration of the venality and passionate defensiveness of the tutors, but by the practical motivation of the pupil. The lessons themselves have their own inner logic as *divertissements* in their own right – *morceaux choisis* that can be easily lifted from context – gratuitous games in which demands and stakes are low (prowess without courage, moral perfection without sacrifice of passions, knowledge without straining mind or taste) so that teacher and pupil are easily served. Monsieur Jourdain has little interest in learning as such except that his own meagre competence in these areas be officially confirmed as "knowledge:" "Cependant je n'ai point étudié, et j'ai fait cela tout du premier coup". (However, I have never studied, and I did that right off the bat.) If, according to Barbara Johnson (1982), L'Ecole des femmes exposes the deceits and self-delusions of the scene of instruction with regard to teachers, Le Bourgeois gentilhomme exposes complacency and inertia with respect to students.

Artistic conventions as well are engagingly exposed during the second act of the comedy, for music is not merely performed for M. Jourdain's transparent pleasure, but it is more realistically offered up to his judgment. Monsieur Jourdain's comments on the *bergeries* in Act I, Scene 2, are benighted and self-contradictory, but they take deadly aim at the pastoral conventions which underlie the courtly ballet. However ridiculous M. Jourdain may be as he removes then dons his robe "pour mieux entendre", (in order to hear better), his judgment may not be too far off the mark when he finds the song "Je languis nuit et jour" "un peu lugubre" (somewhat lugubrious). Jourdain's very solid bourgeois presence, plodding, but not uncurious, calls into question the conventions of amorous pastoral which for centuries had passed for high courtly art. However, his own song with "du mouton dedans" (some sheep in it) is merely another version of pastoral, of a popular sort, so that he himself unwittingly undermines his own pertinent query, "Pourquoi toujours des bergers? On ne voit que cela partout". ("Why are there always shepherds? That's all you ever see".) (I, 2) The dancing master pertinently speaks of "vraisemblance", (plausibility) which supposedly excludes princes and the middle class alike from expressing themselves through song, but the power of realistic middle-class comedy over aristocratic pastoral convention draws even the "Ballet des Nations" into its ambit, especially the "Dialogue des Gens" which has singing roles for a "Femme du bel air" and a "Vieux Bourgeois Babillard".

The presence of art within art is invariably a destabilizing one by virtue of the sharp contrast between the prevailing conventions of representation and another set of artistic conventions associated with the past or with limited, less comprehensive means of representation. From *Les Précieuses ridicules* with Magdelon's detailing in scene 4 of the conventions of pastoral romance (presupposing a knowledge of the rules of the genre that by rights should be critically alienating) to the sonnet/song scene in *Le Misanthrope* and the salon scene of *Les Femmes savantes*, Molière's theatre offers many memorable examples of literary parody and demystification. The *comédie-ballet* genre itself is a hybrid of several arts whose relation to each other becomes increasingly problematic as the walls between the arts and, implicitly, the classes, blur or crumble. The wished for harmony among the arts can be sung (and danced) as they are in the prologue to *L'Amour médecin*, but the moment one art enters the frame of another, ironic discords arise.

This internal commentary on the genre indicates, most likely, an impatience with the genre, and not just on the part of Monsieur Jourdain. Critics habitually speak of Molière's seamless fusion of comedy and ballet (cf. Mazouer, 1993), but, just as in *Les précieuses ridicules*, it is the courtly pastoral conventions which are exposed in their repetitive and simplistic hollowness within the ampler famework of the conventions of comic realism. At the same time, Monsieur Jourdain's impatience with and discomfiture at sung or danced interludes gave Molière the actor the occasion to have comedy intrude upon whatever *divertissement* was at hand. The wedding of comedy and courtly ballet is at best a wish, a pious hope undercut by such indications as the fact that *George Dandin* survives as a purely dramatic text divorced of its musical entra'actes. Nor did the genre survive Molière's demise, but quickly yielded to the rage for the non-critical spectacle of heroic opera.

Whatever faint success the lessons in the arts, arms and philosophy may have, Monsieur Jourdain finally yields, in the concluding balletic scene to the impromptu of Acts I–II, to the outer lure of apparel as an even less demanding way of achieving the social distinction he seeks. As cloth made the Jourdains, so clothes, not education, seemingly make the gentleman. Even so, the comedy of the last scene of the second act has to do with Jourdain responding with coin for each successively ennobling salutation, a cultural-mercantile exchange in which desire for grandeur and gratuities imposes no outward limits until it approaches the tabou threshold of *lèse-majesté*: "Ma foi, s'il va jusqu'à l'Altesse, il aura toute la bourse ... Il a bien fait: je lui allais tout donner". (My goodness, if he goes as far as 'Highness', he'll get all my purse ... Thank God; I was going to give him everything) (II, 5).

It is only with the third act that the flattery and delusions of social *perfectionnement* bought by Monsieur Jourdain in the ludic impromptus of first two acts are punctured (*castigat mores ridendo*) by laughter, but it is telling that the servant Nicole's involuntary laughter is symptomatic of a violation of decorum. It takes the arrival of Mme Jourdain for her to articulate an image of social or moral reality. Even so, the comedy is driven by Monsieur Jourdain's fantasies and arrangements so that the sub-plot involving Dorante's interventions with Dorimène (for a price) takes precedence over a clear exposition of what values and issues are disrupted or threatened by Monsieur Jourdain's extravagant ambitions. In *Le Bourgeois gentilhomme* Molière has inverted the usual structure of his major social comedies: an initial exposition of the persons and interests that are involved in conflict, the representation of the site of contention, household or salon. Although the initial debate between music and dancing masters gives the illusion of a normal exposition, it addresses the marginal, professional question of patronage, a more abstract issue than the survival of the bourgeois household with which the comic plot is concerned.

One has to wait until Act III, scene 12, roughly the center of the act, and thus of the comedy, to find the conflictual expository statements that correspond to the rationally argued interests of the major comedies, the two *Ecoles, Tartuffe, Le Misanthrope*. Here there are two speeches that systematically expose the class system of the Ancien Régime and the possibilities of moving or not moving within it. First, there is Cléonte's astonishingly lucid and straightforward presentation of his social credentials of military service and public office. Cléonte's speech is now a *locus classicus* for social and cultural historians who chart the slow, quiet rise of the wealthiest middle-class families into the established aristocracy though legal farming, exogamy, "living nobly", i.e., refraining from commerce, etc.[4] As Gerhard Gerhardi puts it, if M. Jourdain himself has precocious pretentions to nobility, those claims might be legitimately realized by his great-grandchildren.[5] While not confusing his army career with the claims to belong to the *noblesse d'épée*, Cléonte has had the coarser characteristics of his bourgeois background effaced, presumably by rubbing elbows with aristocratic officers.[6] His speech is full of aristocratic grace that justifiably claims title to *honnêteté* and yet with paradoxical panache and bravura does not mince words about his class origins.

Je suis né de parents, sans doute, qui ont tenu des charges honorables. Je me suis acquis dans les armes l'honneur de six ans de services, et je me trouve assez de bien pour tenir dans le monde un rang assez passable. Mais, avec tout cela, je ne veux point me donner un nom où d'autres en ma place croiraient pouvoir prétendre, et je vous dirai franchement que je ne suis point gentilhomme.

(I was born of parents who certainly held honorable office. I fulfilled honorably six years of military service, and I have enough money to hold a decent rank in society. But

---

[4] See Ellery Schalk, *From Valor to Pedegree: Ideas of Nobility in France in the Sixteenth and Seventeenth Centuries* (Princeton: Princeton University Press, 1986), especially pp. 150, 198–201, and 205 which discuss Clónte's status, and George Huppert, *Les Bourgeois Gentilshommes: An Essay on the Definition of Elites in Renaissance France* (Chicago and London: University of Chicago Press, 1977), where the title no longer has a comic resonance..
[5] Gerhard C. Gerhardi, "Circulation monétaire et mobilité sociale dans le *Bourgeois gentilhomme*", in Kapp, p. 32.
[6] Cf. La Rochefoucauld, "L'air bourgeois se perd quelquefois à l'armée, mais il ne se perd jamais à la cour". *Maxime* 393. Jules Brody cites this stricture, p. 317, but with an eye to the admittedly incorrigible Jourdain. Cléonte's middle-class elegance complicates the play's social representations.

even so, I don't want to pretend to a rank that others in my place might be willing to claim, and I will tell you frankly that I am not a nobleman) (III, 12).

The conclusion of Cléonte's speech is Utopian in the sense that the bourgeois placed like Cléonte's family would be more discreet in blurring their bourgeois and commercial background, Monsieur Jourdain, being a case in point. M. Jourdain's reaction is predictably reductive: "Vous n'êtes point gentilhomme, vous n'aurez pas ma fille" (You are not a nobleman, so you won't marry my daughter) (III, 12).

The second speech of importance in the scene is that of Mme Jourdain and it strikes a very different note. Whereas Cléonte shows to what extent a military career is open to the bourgeois, and to what degree such a career can produce a spirited and graceful elegance that is metaphorically aristocratic in tone, Mme Jourdain's tirade is more narrowly anecdotal and focused on the hypothetical attempt of a woman to rise above her class and the potential ridicule, specifically from her neighbors, that would ensue. Hers is a very vivid and specific scenario, more satiric than "moraliste" and stands to Cléonte's speech as, say, Dorine's specific satire of persons in the first scene of *Tartuffe* to Cléonte's more general moralizing remarks on social hypocrisy.

No less than Cléonte's speech, Mme Jourdain's is a bravura set piece. It begins sententiously and even somewhat preciously: "Les alliances avec plus grand que soi sont sujettes toujours à de fâcheux inconvénients". (Alliances with those socially higher up are always troublesome) (III, 12). But then it becomes local, personal and specific:

Je ne veux point qu'un gendre puisse à ma fille reprocher ses parents, et qu'elle ait des enfants qui aient honte de m'appeler leur grand-maman.
(I don't want my son-in-law to reproach my daughter for her parents, nor that she may have children who are ashamed of their grandma.)

Mme Jourdain continues relentlessly with anguished anecdotes of remarkable specificity that constitute a little social comedy within the comedy:

S'il fallait qu'elle me vînt visiter en équipage de grand-dame, et qu'elle manquât par mégarde à saluer quelqu'un du quartier, on ne manquerait pas aussitôt de dire cent sottises. "Voyez-vous, dirait-on, cette Madame la Marquise qui fait tant la glorieuse? c'est la fille de Monsieur Jourdain, qui était trop heureuse, étant petite, de jouer à la madame avec nous: elle n'a pas toujours été si relevée que la voilà; et ses deux grands-pères vendaient du drap auprès de la porte Saint-Innocent. Ils ont amassé du bien à leurs enfants, qu'ils payent maintenant peut-être bien cher en l'autre monde, et l'on ne devient guère si riches à être honnêtes gens."
(If she had to visit me in a fine carriage, and she happened to forget to greet someone from the neighborhood, they wouldn't fail to voice some foolish criticism: "Do you see, they'd say, Madam the Marquise who is so uppety? She's the daughter of Monsieur Jourdain, who was happy to play the lady: she hasn't always been so high and mighty as

that; and her two grandfathers used to sell cloth near the city gate of St. Innocent. They made their children rich, for which perhaps they are now paying very dearly in the next world, for honest folk hardly become that rich.)

A concluding judgment that looks back to the beginning of her speech and a final positive, homely flourish – in the cadences of a regular *alexandrin*, one is surprised to note – seem guaranteed to elicit a sympathetic response on the part of the spectators:

Je ne veux point tous ces caquets et je veux un homme, en un mot, qui m'ait obligation de ma fille, et à qui je puisse dire: "Mettez-vous là, mon gendre, et dînez avec moi.
 (I don't want all this gossip and I want a man, in short, who is grateful to me to be married to my daughter, and to whom I can say: "Sit there, my son-in-law, and dine with me.)

Mme Jourdain's speech captures all the complex flavor of neighborhood *commérage*, the inconvenient collective memory and anxiety not just of a decade (back to Lucile's childhood), but of generations. It is the objective knowledge and reflection of a community who indiscretely recall the humble trade and (ironic) business address of the grandparents, Molière implicates his own family history in Mme Jourdain's account of her origins, since the dramatist's family business, upholsterery, was located by the Porte Saint-Innocent, which allows us to imagine M. Jourdain's momentary writhing reaction to long and carefully suppressed facts. This evoked collective voice goes on to speculate shrewdly about the moral compromises that may underlie great fortunes; the devoutly cast accusation possibly hints at more precise, criminal details, well-known to the Jourdains. Yet whatever might be said about the Jourdains' origins, the potential skeletons – the "Innocents" was a neighborhood cemetery – in the family closet, they would remain well-kept secrets unless some insolent gesture affronted the self-important cohesiveness of the neighborhood.

This complex prosopopeia – a *que dira-t-on* of remarkable density – shows just how neighborhood/class boundaries are instituted and internalized through recollection and fear. Mme Jourdain is able to visualize just what the uncomfortable consquences of social ambition would be in the eyes of others, not just of those above her socially, but more important, of those of her own social milieu. Mme Jourdain's discourse reveals a structure of social containment that goes beyond superficial values or commitments to explore imaginary scenarios of humiliation and reprisal. It is in fact a dynamic structure of fear, fear particularly of ridicule, but also of reprisal, having one's past thrown up to one, just as one dares make the attempt to dissociate oneself from the neighborhood and class of origin, a trajectory that Molière himself had negotiated. What is shown here is less the wisdom of *bon sens* than how "reality" is socially constructed through hypothetical confrontations of an eminently theatrical sort.

The supressed term of Mme Jourdain's speech of course is "woman". When Cléonte traces his social rise from commerce to military service and public office, without ever disowning his bourgeois background, there is nothing tugging at him, no family ghosts or neighborhood gossip. His success takes place in a social vacuum; when he joins the army, there is no voice to nag that he is getting too big for his social breeches. But when a woman attempts to rise in society by marriage, she is subject to criticism of her pretentions and to threats that the seamier aspects of her background might be disclosed.

Finally, to the assumed voice of the community, Mme Jourdain adds her own concern that she will be snobbishly disdained by her son-in-law who will reject her companionship, her presence at table, the importance of which Ronald Tobin (1990) has recently shown us. Ultimately her fear is that she will be powerless to invite and she will be spurned as lower-class. Invariably it is the woman who receives the burden of class prejudice, while a man like Cléonte has a relative freedom to cross class lines. If he is still a bourgeois in name, he is nevertheless to all appearances an aristocrat. In *Du Mèrite personnel* 25, La Bruyère, a lifelong bachelor, comments upon the social mobility of the aspiring and talented bachelor as opposed the married man whose social position is fixed by that of his wife:

"Un homme libre, et qui n'a point de femme, s'il a quelque esprit, peut s'élever au-dessus de sa fortune, se mêler dans le monde, et aller de pair avec les plus honnêtes gens. Cela est moins facile à celui qui est engagé: il semble que le marriage met tout le monde dans son ordre." A free man who is unmarried, if he has any wit, can rise above his social position, mix with high society, and be on an equal footing with the most distinguished people. That is harder for one who has a wife: it appears that marriage fixes everyone in his station.

M. Jourdain would seem to be instinctively aware of this social law, which would explain in part why he harbors such deep resentment against his wife, one that echoes until the penultimate line of the comedy.

M. Jourdain is as dismissive of his wife's harrangue as he is of Cléonte's discourse; in a scene of bravura outdoing and climaxes, he outdoes his own reductiveness to cap Mme Jourdain's concluding egalitarian gesture with an irate threat of his own that seems to be paradoxically aware of its own madness: "ma fille sera marquise en dépit de tout le monde; et si vous me mettez en colère, je la ferai duchesse" (my daughter will be a marquise in spite of everyone; and if you make me angry, I'll make her a duchess) Jourdain, buffeted by his prospective son-in-law and harridan wife – it should never be forgot that

Mme Jourdain was originally a role played by the actor Hubert in drag, not, as tradition has evolved, by a warmly sympathetic, middle-aged actress – is caught in the toils of history as transitional figure, in his desire to escape the fear-driven conformity of his wife and yet too set in his ways to acquire the virile elegance given to Cléonte by his youthful training.

For all its realistic, homespun, narrow, but experiential focus, its local knowledge and traces of authorial confession, Mme Jourdain's discourse is eminently literary in that it patently echoes a conservative tradition of strongly worded feminine invective aimed at social climbing. Often noted as Molière's model is the vivid scene between Sancho Panza and his wife Teresa in chapter 5 of part II of Cervantes' *Don Quixote*, for there Sancho, still dreaming of becoming the governor of an island hopes that his daughter will by a brilliant marriage become a *señora*, while Teresa is vociferously opposed to her husband's ambitions, an intransegeance that only foments the obsessive social ambitions of the husband. Another passage worth comparing is the similarly energetic and "theatrical" diatribe against unworthy social climbers which provides the scathing and ironic climax to Boccaccio's novella of Arriguccio and Monna Sismonda in the *Decameron* (VII, 8). This is the tale of a *mésalliance* between a merchant who has foolishly wed a noble woman, and how his wife ingeniously tricks her boorish husband so as to carry on a tryst with her lover. As in *George Dandin*, for which it is one of the sources for the opprobrium of the Sottenville's, the guilty wife arranges matters so that it is the innocent husband who bears the blame, which is largely cast in a speech of stunning invective by the wife's mother. What Monna Sismonda's mother's speech shares with Mme Jourdain's is the same lively perspective on class relations seen through the lens of strong feelings, here out and out aristocratic contempt rather than middle-class anxiety. Like Mme Jourdain (and Teresa Panza), the mother similarly constructs a miniature drama with colorful direct discourse.

Monna Sismonda's mother's diatribe sets a pattern for comic realism in European literature. As Boccaccio's text makes clear, and in this he is followed by Cervantes, literary "realism" is generated precisely at the site of contestation between two classes. It is where, out of anxiety, insecurity, pride and contempt, the dominant class, to preserve its identity, angrily disparages with as many damning facts and cruel observations as it can the class that would join and displace it. However, the realistic impulse can be, as in Mme Jourdain's case, just as effectively internalized by the oppressed class or gender. The effect of the real is reinforced by the strong and irrational voice of a woman – yet a woman with virile power – old in years and experience, her back up; intransigent, proud, angry, whose very engery embodies an seemingly unbridgable social barrier. It is not surprising that Molière should have turned to the chief creators of modern European realistic narrative to represent Mme Jourdain's vision of "social reality". That it is *déjà lu*, a derivative, version of a repeated *topos*, accounts for the sense we have of its ritualized solidity, although we may feel that coming as it does after Cléonte's contemporary, quasi-documentary account of his ongoing ascendancy, that it is dated, foreign, indeed more contingent and full of artifice than Mme Jourdain knows.

Authorial psychocriticism is beyond our powers, but it is nevertheless tempting to speculate that Mme Jourdain's borrowed social anxieties represents an anxiety on the part of Molière, not just as a courtly entertainer who has risen from the same bourgeois milieu and trade as the Jourdains, but as a writer who has often stood in debt to the ultramontane comic narrative tradition and specifically to Boccaccio (whether for the intrigue for *L'Ecole des maris, Le Médecin volant, George Dandin* and other borowings), and yet who, along with La Fontaine, urbane translator of many of Boccaccio's *novelle* has displaced Boccaccio as the leading comic realist of his own culture. French literary classicism in great measure depends upon just this literary usurpation of Italian and Spanish literary models which were preeminent particularly in the first half of the seventeenth century. Inveighing against upstarts, can be read as a metaphor for the right of literary place being given to the first to seize it. Molière's Mme Jourdain attempts to dissuade her husband from being an upstart is a secondary formation that bears signs of denial of authorial usurpation.[7] Although Molière's royal command was to provide a comedy with a Turkish theme, orientalism and foreignness in *Le Bourgeois gentilhomme* are, when they are not merely a question of costume, largely an affair of Italian words – above all in the Turkish ceremony in Act IV, but also in the "Quatrième Entrée" of the "Ballet des Nations" (Spanish is used in the "Troisième Entrée") – as if distance were sufficiently represented by difference, a translucency that identifies Italian not just with "foreignness", but with falsity and *divertissement*, corrected by the honest and instructive "truth" of French. In the process, Italian, and to a lesser degree Spanish, lose whatever position they might have had as originary languages and cultures of the modern classic period and as the enduring rival of French for the patronage of Anne of Austria and Cardinal Mazarin, and before them that of Marie de' Médicis., a period examined, among others, by Mousnier and Mesnard (1985).

What throws Mme Jourdain's seemingly realistic vision of immutably fixed class (and neighborhood) boundaries into some doubt is a short, almost off-handed, and critically neglected scene earlier in the act that at

---

[7] This contestatory model of influence is, of course, based on Harold Bloom, *The Anxiety of Influence* (London and New York: Oxford U.P., 1973).

first glance seems merely a filler for M. Jourdain to exit momentarily to find the 200 *pistoles* that the artful Dorante wishes to borrow. Act III, scene 5 finds Mme Jourdain alone with Dorante; it is an uneasy society, and Mme Jourdain responds to Dorante's polite overtures about her seeming unhappiness with sarcastic literalism that recalls Sganarelle's retorts to Martine in the first scene of *Le Médecin malgré lui*. But Dorante gracefully attempts to relieve the tension by inviting Mme Jourdain and her daughter to a royal *divertissement:* "Ne voulez-vous point un de ces jours venir voir, avec elle, le ballet et la comédie que l'on fait chez le Roi?" (Would you not one of these days come to see with her the ballet and comedy that they are performing at court for the King?) (III, 5) Dorante's use of the definite article and present tense implies an immediacy that suggests uncannily that the *comédie-ballet* to which Mme Jourdain is being invited is none other than the play in which she herself is a character, although the vague futurity of the invitation blunts that implication. Without wishing to press this momentary metatheatrical dimension overly, I would merely point out that the conclusion of the play is also ambiguously located in fictional and real time and space. Mme Jourdain refuses brusquely with a succulent, chiastic idiom of popular speech: "Nous avons fort envie de rire, fort envie de rire nous avons". (We really feel like laughing, like really laughing we do.) Dorante pursues in an attempt to remind Mme Jourdain of her youth when she perhaps did not take things so seriously. Mme Jourdain chooses to take this in an unfavorable sense as casting aspersions on her age, while Dorante tries to save the situation by ironically agreeing to her delusions of youth:

DORANTE: Je pense, Madame Jourdain, que vous avez eu bien des amants dans votre jeune âge, belle et d'agréable humeur que vous étiez.
MADAME JOURDAIN: Tredame! monsieur, est-ce que Madame Jourdain est décrépite, et la tête lui grouille-t-elle déjà?
DORANTE: A ma foi, madame Jourdain, je vous demande pardon. Je ne songeais pas que vous êtes jeune, et je rêve le plus souvent. Je vous prie d'excuser mon impertinance.
(DORANTE: I think, Mme Jourdain, that you must have had lots of lovers when you were young, pretty and charming.
MME JOURDAIN: Landsakes! Sir. Is Madam Jourdain so decrepit, and does her head already tremble?
DORANTE: I sincerely beg your pardon, Madam. I didn't think that you are still young; I am very absent-minded. I beg you to excuse my impertinence.)

What might be seen meaningless bantering is belied by Dorante, who repeats the invitation somewhat hyperbolically in the following scene when M. Jourdain returns with the loan: "Si Madame Jourdain veut voir le divertissement royal, je lui ferai donner les meilleures places de la salle". (If Mme Jourdain wants to see the royal spectacle, I will have her given the best places in the theater.) (III, 6). And Mme Jourdain again rejects the offer with more sarcasm: "Madame Jourdain vous baise les mains". (Mme Jourdain takes her leave of you.)

The brief confrontation between Dorante and Mme Jourdain seems to go nowhere, and its implications are highly ambiguous. George Couton is not wrong to see that Dorante's favor is less than it seems since the King's entertainments were not all that exclusive,[8] while Despois and Mesnard cannot be faulted for noting that invitations to Chambord must have been highly selective.[9] In defense of Dorante, it should be observed that he does not present the invitation as a favor, but as an offer to divert Mme Jourdain and her daughter. To be sure, the success of his projects are forwarded by significant absences. But Dorante's invititation can hardly be the exclusive 1670 Chambord ticket. Rather it recalls to some degree the festivities in the gardens of Versailles on July 18, 1668 when royal entertainments were opened to a wider audience by a triumphant, thirty-year-old Louis XIV after the conquest of the Franche-Comté.[10] Rather than reserving the entertainments for his own class, Dorante shares them with the Jourdains fully in the spirit of the King's paradigmatic magnanimity. Dorante is clearly an agent of a royal politics of culture that imposes its hegemony of representation not merely on the aristocracy, but the bourgeoisie as well. Corresponding to no precise occasion. however, Dorante's invitation is an ideological gesture that represents court spectacle as an experience that can be enjoyed in common by both classes, even if centered around the glory of the king. The invitation implies that the theatre itself, unlike M. Jourdain's illusory visions of social ascendancy, offers an imaginative escape from the limitations of middle-class practicality, that it is allied not merely with royal and aristocratic prerogatives, but with common experiences like youth and love. As I have argued (Berk, 1972), art, and specifically the theatre, has a therapeutic value in Le Malade imaginaire. The theatre in Le Bourgeois gentilhomme would seem likewise to represent a socially transcendant site, where class divisions and interests are momentarily forgot in the mutual pursuit or nostaligic recovery of pleasure in the private sphere, and in the affirmation of royal prerogative in the public sphere.

---

[8] Couton, p. 1428.
[9] Despois and Mesnard, p. 121.
[10] "Un deuxième dèplacement s'introduit entre 1664 et 1668. Le 18 juillet<1668>, les invités du roi appartiennent à tous les ordres de la société, élargissant la nation au-delà du cercle de la noblesse. Ils ne se déguisent pas en chevaliers d'épopée mais en membres lumineux du corps du roi." Apostolidès, p. 110.

Mme Jourdain simply refuses to listen to Dorante's effort to cajole and flatter her out of her hard-headed resistance to his presence or to his offer of theatrical entertainment. Presumably this resistance is founded on an aversion to laughter, and Mme Jourdain's long diatribe in Act III, scene 12 offers an explanation for her aversion, since it is precisely laughter as mockery, the ridicule of neighbors, which Mme Jourdain knows and fears. This is the cold-hearted, self-exempting laughter of Sganarelle in *L'Ecole des maris* or of Arnolphe in *L'Ecole des femmes*, not the urbane, reflexive laughter that Molière has Uranie describe in *La Critique de l'Ecole des femmes* in which satire takes its aim only in an indirect way that allows the members of the audience not to have to confess publically to its accuracy:

Ces sortes de satires tombent directement sur les moeurs, et ne frappent les personnes que par réflexion. N'allons point nous appliquer nous-mêmes les traits d'une censure générale; et profitons de la leçon, si nous pouvons, sans faire semblant qu'on parle à nous.

(These sorts of satires fall directly on manners, and strike individuals only upon reflection. Let us not apply to ourselves the outlines of a general censure; and let us profit from the lesson, if we can, without making it appear that they are speaking to us.) (scene 6).

That the theater might be kindly and reflexive rather than cruel and blunt is presumably above Mme Jourdain's sights. It is nor surprising that Mme Jourdain is therefore so recalcitrant during the Turkish ceremony of Act IV to see that the episode is a fabulation to deceive her husband so that the young lovers can triumph over his mania. She is like Mme Pernelle in *Tartuffe*, the most ardent believer, ironically the voice of radical scepticism, the last to be persuaded as to the truth of Tartuffe's character. Her imagination frozen by the fear of social ridicule, Mme Jourdain's philistinism makes it almost impossible for her to understand a "theatrical" and indirect way of triumphing over M. Jourdain's obsession with nobility, even though her own brand of confrontation and ridicule has borne no fruit. This theatrical indirection is precisely what Elmire is able to muster so as to convince Orgon to overcome his blindness to Tartuffe, and equally what enables Argan to sort out the truth and falsity of his household. The elaborate *turquerie* is usually explained as a necessary blinding of M. Jourdain so that as a counterfeit nobleman he can participate in the balletic *dénouement*, but it is perhaps even more important that Mme Jourdain be inducted into the role of theater and good-willed dissimulation in everyday life so that she can concur in the final duping of her husband as the only solution to the plot's impasse.

The action of the comedy, insofar as the comedy is a prologue to the ballet to come, is to move by degrees the entire Jourdain family to the royal stage so that they can as spectators establish the transition between comedy and courtly ballet. Just as Oronte's family in *Tartuffe* must be united against the imposter so as to be worthy of the king's all-seeing justice, so the Jourdains must be as one to merit attendance at a royal spectacle. Helen Purkis (1980) reads the "Ballet des Nations" as the crowning feature of the spectacle which allows Dorante to woo Dorimène in music and dance and to satirize the bourgeoisie on whom he is momentarily financially dependent , as well as to connect with the aristocratic self-image of the courtly audience. These comments do not sufficiently underscore the ambiguous status of the concluding "Ballet des Nations' as not just the fictional *divertissement* promised during the comedy, but as the royal *divertissement* presented by Louis XIV to his court. Dorante's invitation of Mme Jourdain and her family to attend a court spectacle initiates that very ambiguity, since the final spectacle must by its hyperbole, palatial luxury and royal ambition far surpass anything that a bourgeois *or* aristocrat could offer to his domestic guests, an issue of artistic patronage that was settled after Nicolas Fouquet's notoriously magnificent festivities at Vaux-le-Vicomte in August, 1661.

I do not believe that it has been sufficiently observed that the note of financial moderation, for all but royal expenses, in matters of spectacle and outward show is struck in the comedy by the sympathetic, worldly widow, Dorimène at the outset. Although no prude since she is attracted to the banquets and theatricals that Dorante manages to arrange on her behalf, Dorimène is anxious about both the dangers of financial ruin for Dorante and the power of spectacle to pursuade beyond the claims of reason, a "baroque" theme dear to Montaigne and Pascal and the very ground of Louis XIV's commitment to spectacle as a persuasive political instrument.

Enfin j'en reviens toujours là: les dépenses que je vous vois faire pour moi m'inquiètent par deux raisons: l'une, qu'elles m'engagent plus que je ne voudrais; et l'autre, que je suis sûre, sans vous déplaire, que vous ne les faites point, que vous ne vous incommodiez; et je ne veux point cela.

(Finally, I come back to that point: the expenses that I see you make for me disturb me for two reasons: first, that they commit me more than I should wish; and second, that I am sure that your expenses must be beyond your means, and I don't want that.) (III, 15, 758).

It is astonishing that an aristocratic woman should voice such a concern about expenditures, but this well accords with the frankness about money that is a chief characteristic of a comedy more often praised for its qualities of fantasy and dream. [11] Dorimène's anxiety about Dorante's prodigality surfaces again in Act V, scene 2, although with a gracefulness that preserves Dorante's self-respect:

---

[11] Curiously, Gerhardi, p. 23, states that in the comedy, the circulation of money is not explicitly thematized.

J'ai vu là des apprêts magnifiques, et ce sont de choses, Dorante, que je ne puis plus souffrir. Oui, je veux enfin vous empêcher vos profusions; et, pour rompre le cours à toutes les dépenses que je vous voir faire pour moi, j'ai résolu de me marier promptement avec vous: c'en est le vrai secret, et toutes ces choses finissent avec le mariage.

(I have seen some magnificent preparations there, and those are things, Dorante, that I can no longer bear. Yes, I want at last to prevent your lavishness; and, in order to stem this flow of all these expenses that I see you make for me, I have resolved to marry you at once: that's the real secret of it, and all things things finish with marriage.) (V, 2).

This entire scene can be read as an example of how an "ideal" marriage has to be regarded both as a financial and emotional partnership, analogous to the way that patronage is understood by the dancing and music masters at the outset of the comedy as a combination of appreciation and financial support. If Dorante gallantly pays more attention to the sentimental side of Dorimène, she proves to be the more pragmatic of the two:

DORANTE: Ah! Madame, est-il possible que vous ayez pu prendre pour moi une si douce résolution?
DORIMENE: Ce n'est que pour vous empêcher de vous ruiner; et, sans cela, je vois bien qu'avant qu'il fût peu, vous n'auriez pas un sou.
DORANTE: Que j'ai d'obligation, Madame aux soins que vous avez de conserver mon bien! Il est entièrement à vous, aussi bien que mon coeur, et vous en userez de la façon qu'il vous plaira.
DORIMENE: J'userai bien de tous les deux.
(DORANTE: Ah! Madam, is it possible that you can have taken so kind a decision towards me?
DORIMENE: It is only to prevent you from ruining yourself; and, without this, I can see that in short order you would not have a penny to your name.
DORANTE: How obliged I am to you, Madam, for your concern for my wealth. It is entirely yours, as is my heart, and you may do with them what you will.
DORIMENE: And so I shall to both of them.)

These personal exchanges are not without their political and social ramifications, for just as Mme Jourdain is, as it were, converted to theater by the Turkish ceremony, so Dorante is presumably converted by Dorimène to financial judiciousness, a chiastic aristocratization of the bourgoisie and a bourgeoisification of the aristocracy, a just reordering of taste and wealth within society that enables the King to effect the classical cultural politics that he and Colbert so brilliantly conceived, to wit, to become sole benefactor and impresario for the nation as a whole. Furthermore, Dorimène's premature acceptance of Dorante obviates, from within the comedy, the original intention of the concluding ballet as an instrument of persuasion on Dorante's part.

The movement of the "Ballet des Nations" is from satire of the vulgar bourgeois spectators (who bear little relation, nevertheless, to the Jourdains) to the praise of the pleasures of the gods, a term that is blasphemous in seventeenth-century ideology unless associated with Louis XIV and the innermost circle of his court. When M. Jourdain urges the company to find their places he is *at once* about to see Dorante's entertainment, which he believes is his own, and to be an unwitting spectator of (and marginal attraction at) a royal *divertissement*. Consequently Dorante's invitation to Mme Jourdain in III, v, is pivotal. Important too is the "metatheatrical" sarcasm of Mme Jourdain: "Je viens de voir un théâtre là-bas." (I have just seen a theatrical performance down there.) (IV, 2). The final movement is from a household theatrically transformed via the Turkish ceremony to an ambiguous liminal moment when the family is gathered as spectators presumably to watch the *divertissement* that Dorante had arranged for M. Jourdain to bestow upon Dorimène, although meant to be understood as his own gift to the marquise, but which ultimately reveals itself by its elaborate scope to be none other than the royal *divertissement* to which Dorante had promised to take Mme Jourdain. This subtle move from household to royal stage establishes the transition between comedy and ballet. It additionally redeems Dorante, if that were necessary, since his role is as a surrogate for the King.

This is a magical moment because until now the musical *divertissement* was anticipated as taking place in M. Jourdain's own house by virtue of the rule of the unities of time and place. Yet the moment that the ballet begins, the very dimensions of the spectacle remind us with a special force that the initial theatrical illusion of of being witness to the goings-on of a bourgeois Parisan household no longer holds, and that we are at Chambord or Saint-Germain or Versailles at the invitation of and in the presence of the King. Utopic mimesis folds into the locative royal spectacle. The Jourdains and their problems are forgot in the spectacle of which "they" and we are the spectators. To that extent, the reality of M. Jourdain's social position and his fantasies of social elevation and amorous intrigue are all momentarily resolved and accomodated by the Jourdains' absorption, although *qua* bourgeois, into the ambit of royal hospitality and into the king's public body, precisely, *la Nation*. The spectacle that we are watching, the invitation to which was foolishly resisted by Mme Jourdain, is testimony to Louis XIV's supreme ability as *Roi-Soleil* and *Roi-Machine*. But the magical moment of the royal ballet is already put into question by its ambivalent five-act comic introduction, for the seemingly miraculous royal ballet is already exposed, within the comedy, as the result of the unwitting complex alliance between the wealth and aspirations of the middle class and the taste and intrigues of the nobility.

The ballet itself continues this metatheatrical framing in its first *entrée* which shows a "multitude de gens" (many people) as rowdy, self-centered spectators who throng the distributor of programs for their copy. Just as the opening scenes of the comedy thematize artistic patronage, so the first scene of the ballet thematizes spectatorship – not perhaps without cause since the royal spectacles had been recently and problematically opened up to a larger public – while the second *entrée* sets the "Importuns" to dancing, at once a retrospective glance to *Les Fâcheux*, the first of the *comédies-ballets* and a transition from spectatorly disorder to order so that the subsequent regal feast, the multi-lingual *entrées* of the nations, can be properly savored.

Nor is the magic of spectacle totally successful in resolving conflicts on all levels. It is no wonder that M Jourdain's final remark – "et <je donne> ma femme à qui la voudra" (and <I give> my wife to anyone who will have her) (V, 6) – unpurged of anger and disgruntlement, represents his wife as the ball and chain that detracts from the achieved felicity and the charmed circle of universal reasonableness, music and dance, nobility, in short, of imaginative integration and theater that prevails at the end of the comedy. It is a burlesque and farcical remark – not unlike Sganarelle's threat to his wife at the end of *Le Médecin malgré lui* – that pierces through the ultimate unreality of the ballet as a symbolic *dénouement*. As long as Mme Jourdain is present, she ineluctably links M. Jourdain to the bourgeoisie and to the hell of farce, not the paradise of spectacle and courtly society. It will take all of the "Ballet des Nations" to lift Jourdain and company to a position where the social and cultural distinction between bourgeois and noble is artistically and poltically transcended in an apotheosis worthy of princes and of course only created by and for Louis XIV.

This final *glissement* whereby a bourgeois/aristocratic entertainment that concludes the comedy reveals itself to be a grand royal entertainment which allows the presence of the aristocracy and the bourgeoisie (all admiring the spectacle of the king admiring the spectacle) is not entirely without parallel in Molière's theater. In *La Comtesse d'Escarbagnas* (1672), the "comédie", a popourri of successful scenes from previous *comédie-ballets* that the eponymous provincial lady believes is being offered to her is in fact destined for the gallant Vicomte's beloved Julie, who remarks: "Je ne doute point qu'elle ne soit allée par la ville se faire honneur de la comédie que vous me donnez sous son nom". (I am sure that she has gone around town boasting of the comedy that you are giving me under her name) (I, i). But the *Comédie-ballet*, a bastard genre transitional between the court ballet and the opera that soon was to overwhelm it, was born in a moment of ambiguous paternity and literal "diversion" that smacks of usurpation and betrayal. For symbolic of the changed nature of patronage in the second half of the seventeenth century is the problematic way, in the titles and prefaces to *Les Fâcheux* (1661), the first of the *comédie-ballets*, that Molière, insisting upon his responsiveness to that first precious moment of royal command, the young King's private request to compose another "fâcheux.", (bore) gets down to business, erasing any sign of his original patron, the *surintendant des Finances*, Nicolas Fouquet, to proclaim that the play was "faite pour les divertissements du Roi" (written for the King's entertainments). In *Le Bourgeois gentilhomme*. the history of the genre plays itself out before us for both Jourdain and Dorante of the comedy are ultimately finessed by the King in the ballet.

References

Apostolidès, Jean-Marie (1981) *Le Roi-Machine: spectacle et politique au temps de Louis XIV*. Paris: Les Editions de Minuit

Berk, Philip (1972) "The Therapy of Art in *Le Malade imaginaire*", *French Review* 45, 39–48

Johnson, Barbara (1982) "Teaching Ignorance: *L'Ecole des femmes*", Yale French Studies 63, 166–182

Mazouer, Charles (1993) *Molière et ses comédies-ballets*. Paris: Klincksieck

Mousnier, Roland and Jean Mesnard (1985) *L'Age d'or du mécénat (1598–1661)* Paris: CNRS

Purkis, Helen M.C. (1980) 'M. Jourdain, Dorante and the 'Ballet des Nations', *Studi Francesi* 24, 224–233

Stenzel, Harmut (1991) "Projet critique et diverstissement de cour: Sur la place de la comédie-ballet et du *Bourgeois gentilhomme* dans le théâtr de Molière", in Volker Kapp, ed. *Le Bourgeois gentilhomme: Problèmes de la comédie-ballet*. Paris, Seattle, Tübingen: Papers on French Seventeenth-Century Literature, pp. 9–22

Tobin, Ronald W. (1990) *Tarte à la crème: Comedy and Gastronomy in Molière's Theater*. Columbus: Ohio State University Press

Notes on Contributors

Philip R. Berk is an Associate Professor of French Literature at the University of Rochester. He has written on Dante, Molière, La Bruyère, Racine, Baudelaire and Renaissance iconography. He has been a fellow at the National Humanities Center. For the past three years he has conducted a seminar in Paris on Molière's major comedies for the Summer Seminar for School Teachers program of the National Endowment for the Humanities.

Peter W. Ferran is Associate Professor of Fine Arts (Theatre) in the College of Liberal Arts at Rochester Institute of Technology. His book, *Performing Brecht: Early Epic Method, 1918–1938*, will be published next year by Southern Illinois University Press. He was co-founder of the Brecht Company in Ann Arbor, Michigan.

Helen L. Harrison is Assistant Professor of French at Moran State University. She received her Ph.D. from Columbia University. Her research and publications have focused on seventeenth-century French theatre, particularly on the textual interplay of money and language as media of exchange and as indicators of social status. She is currently finishing a book, *Pistoles/Paroles: Money and Language in Seventeenth-Century French Comedy*.

Laurence Romero is Professor of French at Villanova University near Philadelphia. His main research interests are modern theatre, theatre production criticism, and performance. He has published a book on Molière criticism and essays on Molière, Racine, Roger Planchon, Robert Wilson, and Claus Peymann, and on decentralization and classical stagings, among others.

Michael Spingler is Associate Professor of French and Adjunct in Theatre Arts at Clark University. He is also Associate Director of Clark's Center for Contemporary Performance. Professor Spingler has directed numerous plays in French and English and his publications include studies on Molière, Jarry, Ionesco, and Anouilh.

Index

actors: in Berliner Ensemble, 19, 19n, 22, 24, 25, 36; in Brechtian adaptation of *Dom Juan*, 19, 22, 24, 25, 36; and epic playing, 36–37; for Planchon production of *L'Avare*, 50, 51, 51n, 52; in Rostock production of *Dom Juan*, 29
adaptations, authorship of, 14–15, 14n
L'Age d'or, 3
L'Amour médecin (Molière), 62
Andromaque (Racine), 3
Anne of Austria, 68
Antigone (Sophocles), 14, 37
Apostolidès, Jean-Marie, 43n, 44, 46, 60, 70n10
Aristotle, 48n12, 54n16
Les Atrides, 3
audience: for Brechtian adaptation of *Dom Juan*, 35, 39; for *L'Avare*, 43, 45–47, 49–51, 54; and money in the theatre, 52–55; Planchon on, 52n; for royal entertainment under Louis XIV, 70; for Théâtre National Populaire (TNP), 52–53, 52n
L'Avare (Molière): audience of, 43, 45–47, 49–51; cast for Planchon production of, 50, 51, 51n, 52; ending of, 45–47, 50–52; lavish staging of, 52; Planchon's production of, 41–42, 49–55; prose writing style of, 47; theme of money in, 41–55

"Ballet des Nations," in *Le Bourgeois Gentilhomme*, 58–59, 71–72, 74–76
Barthes, Roland, 8
Bénichou, Paul, 10, 43n, 44n6
Bentley, Eric, 14n
Bérénice (Racine), 2, 5–8, 41n
Berk, Philip R., 57–76, 77
Berliner Ensemble: adaptions of European drama by, 14, 19n, 20, 37; authorship question of adaptations for, 14–15, 14n; and Brechtian adaptation of *Dom Juan*, 13–39; cast for *Dom Juan*, 19, 22, 24, 25, 36; comic-critical interpretation of *Dom Juan* by, 17–18; dramaturgical discussion of *Dom Juan*, 17, 19–25, 21n; early productions of, 19, 19n; and epic playing, 36–37; performance of Brechtian *Dom Juan*, 25–35; permanent repertory of, 37; reasons for choice of *Dom Juan*, 15–16, 19–20, 37; and theatrical revision of mythic Don Juan, 35–39
Berliner Ensemble Bearbeitungen, 14
Besson, Benno, 14n, 16, 17–19, 19n, 20, 24, 33

Boccaccio, 67, 68
Bourdieu, Pierre, 42
Le Bourgeois Gentilhomme (Molière): art within art in, 61–62; artistic conventions exposed in, 61; "Ballet des Nations" in, 71–72, 74–76; Cléonte's speech in, 63–64; comparison among the arts in, 60–61; conflictual expository statements in, 63–68; confrontation between Dorante and Mme Jourdain, 68–71; first performance of, 57, 59, 60; Lully's music for, 58–59; Mme Jourdain's speech in, 64–68; opening tableau of, 58; rehearsal–performance structure of, 58–59; theme of work and its monetary rewards in, 57–76; title of, 58
bourgeoisie, 43–46, 60, 64, 74–75
Brecht, Bertolt: and adaptation of *Dom Juan*, 13–39, 14n; adaptations of European drama, 14, 19n, 20, 37; and Berliner Ensemble's dramaturgical discussion of *Dom Juan*, 17, 19–25, 21n; on comedy, 21–22, 21n; and comic technique in *Dom Juan*, 15–39; on "Dialectic" theatre, 39; on epic playing, 36–37, 39; and *Der Kaukasische Kreidekreis* production, 19n; on new theatre's goals, 35; and performance of Brechtian adaptation of *Dom Juan*, 25–35; Potts on, 28n; principle of *Historisierung*, 16, 16n; and question of authorship of *Dom Juan* adaptation, 14–15, 14n; and "socially comic," 16, 25, 36, 38; and theatrical revision of mythic Don Juan, 35–39; on traditional comedy, 21
Brody, Jules, 58n2
Bunge, Hans, 19, 22

Cartoucherie de Vincennes, 3
Cervantes, 67
Chappuzeau, Samuel, 49
character types, 20, 35–39
Chéreau, Patrice, 1, 2, 4
Chirac, Jacques, 51
Christian, Norbert, 19, 19n, 24, 29
classical theatre: Brechtian version of *Dom Juan*, 13–39; contemporary stagings of, 2–10; teaching of, 1–2
comédie-ballet genre, 57–58, 61–62, 69, 75–76
comedy: Berliner Ensemble's *commedia*-style routines in *Dom Juan*, 26–35;. Brecht on traditional comedy, 21; Brechtian idea of "the socially comic," 16, 25, 36, 38; and

79

character types, 20, 35–39; *Dom Juan* as, 15–39; and emergence of bourgeoisie, 20; Marx's ideas on, 36n; Moliére as comedian, 21n; Molière's traditional comic features of *Dom Juan*, 25–35; neo-classical comedy of Molière, 20–21; physical comedy, 29
commedia dell'arte, 15–16, 19, 26, 27, 29–32
La Comtesse d'Escarbagnas (Molière), 75
Copfermann, Emile, 2, 7
Coriolanus (Shakespeare), 14, 37
Corneille, Pierre, 42
Corneille, Thomas, 21
Corvin, Michel, 2, 52n
costumes, in *Dom Juan*, 33
Cournot, Michel, 51n, 52
courtly life, 7, 20, 23, 42–43
Couton, George, 70
La Critique de l'Ecole des femmes (Molière), 71

Daoust, Yvette, 41n, 51, 52
Decameron (Boccaccio), 67
Despois, Eugère, 59n3, 70
Dessau, Paul, 14
Dessert, Daniel, 44n7
deus ex machina, 9–10
Deutsches Theater, 19
"Dialectic" theatre, 39
directors: of Berliner Ensemble, 14n, 16, 17–19, 19n; Besson and Brechtian adaptation of *Dom Juan*, 14n, 16, 17–19, 20, 33; and contemporary stagings of the classics, 2; innovative French directors since 1950, 2–4. *See also* specific directors
Dom Juan (Molière): ancient régime society in, 2; atheism of Don Juan in, 18, 23–24; authorship of Brechtian adaptation of, 14–15, 14n; band of oarsmen in, 31–32; banning of, 21; Berliner Ensemble's dramaturgical discussion of, 17, 19–25, 21n; Besson's director's notes for Berliner Ensemble *Program*, 17–18, 17n; Brechtian version of, for Berliner Ensemble, 13–39, 14n; cast of Brechtian version of, 19, 22, 24, 25, 36; casting of, by Molière, 18; Chéreau's production of, 1, 4–5; as comedy, 15–39; comic-critical interpretation of, by Berliner Ensemble, 17–18; Corneille version of, 21; costumes in, 33; criticism of Brechtian version of, 16–17; dialectical interplay between low comic and "Epic" devices of performances, 26–35; Doctor Marphurius in, 26, 29–30; Don Juan's father in, 31–32; ending of, 18, 22–23, 32–35; first monologue by Don Juan, 27–28; Molière's difficulties in writing and staging, 21; old interpretations of, 16; opening scene of, 26–27; performance of Brechtian adaptation of, 25–35; reasons for inclusion in Berliner Ensemble's project, 15–16, 19–20, 37; Rostock production of, 23, 28, 29, 33; set design of Brechtian version of, 26; Sganarelle in, 26–32, 34; switching costumes in, 30–31; theatrical revision of mythic Don Juan by Brecht, 35–39
Don Giovanni (Mozart), 32, 34, 38
Don Quixote (Cervantes), 67
Dort, Bernard, 2, 5–6
Die Dreigroschenoper (Brecht), 19
Du Mèrite personnel (La Bruyère), 66
dueling, 30
Dumur, Guy, 52

L'Ecole des femmes (Molière), 46, 61, 63, 71
L'Ecole des maris (Molière), 59, 63, 68, 71
écriture scénique, 1
epic playing: and Berliner Ensemble's aim, 39; Brecht on, 36–37; dialectical interplay between low comic and, in *Dom Juan*, 26–35, 38
Epic theatre, 13–39
L'Etourdi (Molière), 46

Les Fâcheux (Molière), 75, 76
Farquhar, George, 14, 19, 20, 37
Faust (Goethe), 34, 38
Les Femmes savantes (Molière), 61
Ferran, Peter W., 13–39, 77
film versus theatre, 52, 53
Fontenelle, Bernard Le Bovier de, 42
Fouquet, Nicolas, 72, 76
Les Fourberies de Scapin (Molière), 46
Fuegi, John, 14n

Gaines, James F., 43
George Dandin (Molière), 41n, 62, 67, 68
Gerhardi, Gerhard, 44, 63, 63n5, 72n
Germany, in 17th century, 20
Geschonneck, Erwin, 19, 19n, 22, 24, 25, 36
Giese, Peter Christian, 17, 36n
Girardot, Annie, 52
Goethe, 16n, 19, 34, 37, 38
Goldoni, Carlo, 32
Goldsmith, Ulrich, 16–17
Grabbe, Christian Dietrich, 38
Gramont, Scipion de, 48n12
Greenblatt, Stephen, 47n10
Grimarest, Jean-Léonor le Gallois, sieur de, 47
Grimm, Reinhold, 16
Grüber, K.-M., 8
Der Gute Mensch von Sezuan (Brecht), 19
Guy, Jean-Michel, 42, 53, 53n, 54

Harrison, Helen L., 41–55, 77
Hauptmann, Elisabeth, 13, 14n

Herr Puntila und Sein Knecht Matti (Brecht), 19, 19n, 21, 36
Hill, Hainer, 26
Historisierung principle, 16, 16n
Hoffmann, Ernst Theodor, 38

Ihering, Herbert, 36n

Johnson, Barbara, 61

kabuki Shakespeare, 3
Der Kaukasische Kreidekreis (Brecht), 19n
Kierkegaard, Soren, 38
Kleist, Heinrich von, 19, 19n, 20, 37
Knopf, Jan, 14–15, 27, 29, 34
Kott, Jan, 10
Krafft, Erich, 29
Kraus, Werner, 21n
Kusche, Lothar, 29, 33

La Bruyère, 5, 66
La Fontaine, 68
La Grange, Charles de, 18, 47n9
La Rochefoucauld, 63n6
Lenz, Jakob, 14, 37
Leonhardt, Gustav, 59
Lessing, Gotthold Ehpraim, 24
Lough, John, 45
Louis XIII, 7
Louis XIV, 2, 7, 9, 20, 23, 26, 33, 70, 72, 74, 75
Lully, Jean-Baptiste, 14, 21, 58–60

Le Malade imaginaire (Molière), 70
Mandel, Oscar, 37n
Manheim, Ralph, 14
Maréchal, Marcel, 2, 4
Marivaux, Pierre Carlet de Chamblain de, 3
Marx, Karl, 36, 36n, 39, 54n
Mazarin, Cardinal, 68
Mazouer, Charles, 62
Le Médecin malgré lui (Molière), 69, 75
Le Médecin volant (Molière), 68
Médicis, Marie de, 68
Mesnard, Jean, 68, 70
Mesward, Paul 59N3, 70
Minna von Barnhelm (Lessing), 24
Le Misanthrope (Molière), 2, 5, 42n3, 59, 61, 63
mises-en-scène, 1–10
Mnouchkine, Ariane, 2, 3
Mogador, 53
Molière: A New Criticism (Moore), 38n
Molière: *Le Bourgeois Gentilhomme* by, 57–76; Brechtian version of *Dom Juan* for Berliner Ensemble, 13–39; as comedian, 21n; comic technique of, in *Dom Juan*, 15–16, 18–26; critics on subtle satire in, 37–38, 38n; difficulties on writing and staging *Dom Juan*, 21; neoclassical comedy of, 20–21; Planchon's production of *L'Avare*, 41–55; Planchon's production of *Tartuffe*, 5, 8–10; social anxieties of, 68; structure of social comedies of, 62–63; and uproar concerning *Tartuffe*, 21; use of prose in plays by, 47, 47n9; Vincent's production of *Le Misanthrope*, 5. *See also* specific plays
Molière (film), 3
money: in *L'Avare*, 41–55, in the theatre, 41–55; work and monetary rewards in *Le Bourgeois Gentilhomme*, 57–76
Moore, W. G., 38n
Morales du grand siècle (Bènichou), 10
Mousnier, Roland, 68
Mozart, Amadeus, 32, 34, 38
Mutter Courage und Ihre Kinder (Brecht), 19, 19n
mythic heroes, 35–39

neoclassical comedy of Molière, 20–21
Neresheimer, Eugen, 14, 14n
New Historicism, 3–4
nobility, 42 49, 74–75

pastoral conventions, 61–62
Pauken und Trompeten (Brecht), 19
Pavis, Patrice, 2
Phèdre (Racine), 3
physical comedy, 29
Piemme, J. M., 2
Planchon, Roger: on the audience, 52n; contributions of, 2, 4; production of *Bérénice*, 5–8; production of *L'Avare*, 41–55; production of *Tartuffe*, 5, 8–10, 51
Potts, D. C., 28n, 38n
Les Précieuses ridicules (Molière), 61, 62
prose, in Molière's plays, 47, 47n9
Der Prozess der Jeanne d'Arc zu Rouen (Seghers), 19n
Puntila (Brecht), 19, 19n, 21, 36
Purkis, Helen, 72

Racine, Jean, 3, 41n
Recruiting Officer, The (Farquhar), 14, 19
Reichel, Käthe, 19, 24
La Rhétorique publicitaire du théâtre, 53–54
Robinet, Charles, 47
Romero, Laurence, 1–10, 77
Rostock production of *Dom Juan*, 23, 28, 29, 33
Rülicke, Käthe, 19, 22, 23

Sandier, Gilles, 2
Savary, Jérôme, 2, 4
Schalk, Ellery, 63n4
Schall, Ekkehard, 24
Seghers, Anna, 14, 19, 19n, 37

Serrault, Michel, 50, 51, 51n, 52, 54
Servant of Two Masters, The (Goldoni), 32
set design: for *L'Avare*, 52; of Brechtian version of *Dom Juan*, 26
1793, 3
1789, 3
Shakespeare, William, 3, 10, 14, 37
Shakespeare our Contemporary (Kott), 10
Simmel, George, 48n12
Simon, Alfred, 2
Sobel, Bernard, 2, 4
social classes: in *L'Avare*, 41–55; in *Le Bourgeois Gentilhomme*, 63–70, 74
"socially comic," 16, 25, 36, 38
Sophocles, 14, 37
Spingler, Michael K., 38n, 77
Stanton, Domna 48n11
Stenzel, Harmut, 57
Subiotto, Arrigo, 17

Tallemant des Réaux, Gédéon, 42
Tartuffe (Molière): ban on, lifted, 9; banning of, 9, 21; compared with *Le Bourgeois Gentilhomme*, 63, 64, 71–72; ending of, 2, 9–10; Molière's three versions of, 9; Orgon's latent homosexuality in, 8–9; Planchon's staging of, 5, 8–10, 41n, 51; uproar concerning, 21
teaching of classical French theatre, 1–2
Theater am Schiffbauerdamm, 13–14
theatre collectives, 3
Théâtre de la Porte Saint-Martin, 51
Théâtre National Populaire (TNP), 5, 52–53, 52n

theatrical production: Brechtian adaptation of *Dom Juan*, 25–35; Chéreau's production of *Dom Juan*, 1, 4–5; contemporary stagings of classical French theatre, 2–10; Planchon's production of *L'Avare*, 41–42, 49–55; Planchon's production of *Tartuffe*, 5, 8–10, 41n, 51; Planchon's staging of *Bérénice*, 5–8; Rostock production of *Dom Juan*, 23, 28, 29, 33; Vincent's *Le Misanthrope*, 5. *See also* specific plays
theatricality, 42–43, 45–48, 47n10
Threepenny Opera, The (Brecht), 27, 33, 34, 35
Tirso, 23
TNP (Théâtre National Populaire), 5, 52–53, 52n
Tobin, Ronald, 66
Trial of Joan of Arc at Rouen (Seghers), 14
Tutor, The (Lenz), 14

Ubersfeld, Anne, 2
Urfaust (Goethe), 16n, 19, 37

Vilar, Jean, 3, 5
Vilar, Pierre, 44n7
Vincent, Jean-Pierre, 2, 4, 5
Vitez, Antoine, 2, 3, 8

Wagnerian operas, 34
Whitton, David, 39n
Willett, John, 14
Wyss, Monika, 29

Zanger, Abby E., 42n4
Der Zerbrochene Krug (Kleist), 19, 19n

For Product Safety Concerns and Information please contact our EU representative GPSR@taylorandfrancis.com
Taylor & Francis Verlag GmbH, Kaufingerstraße 24, 80331 München, Germany

www.ingramcontent.com/pod-product-compliance
Lightning Source LLC
Chambersburg PA
CBHW031714230426
43668CB00006B/211